100 Ideas for Primary Teachers:

Supporting Pupils with Social, Emotional and Mental Health Difficulties

Roy Howarth

BLOOMSBURY EDUCATION

LONDON OXFORD NEW YORK NEW DELHI SYDNEY

BLOOMSBURY EDUCATION
Bloomsbury Publishing Plc
50 Bedford Square, London, WC1B 3DP, UK

BLOOMSBURY, BLOOMSBURY EDUCATION and
the Diana logo are trademarks of Bloomsbury Publishing Plc

First published in Great Britain, 2019 by Bloomsbury Publishing Plc

A catalogue record for this book is available from the British Library

ISBN: PB: 978-1-4729-6161-7; ePDF: 978-1-4729-6160-0;
ePub: 978-1-4729-6159-4

2 4 6 8 10 9 7 5 3 1

Typeset by Newgen KnowledgeWorks Pvt. Ltd., Chennai, India
Printed and bound in the UK by CPI Group (UK) Ltd., Croydon, CR0 4YY

MIX
Paper from
responsible sources
FSC
www.fsc.org
FSC® C013604

All papers used by Bloomsbury Publishing Plc are natural, recyclable products
from wood grown in well managed forests. The manufacturing processes
conform to the environmental regulations of the country of origin

To find out more about our authors and books visit
www.bloomsbury.com and sign up for our newsletters

Contents

Introduction

Children with SEMH can be extremely difficult, every day, and will always be with us in the classroom. They seem to resist learning; they search for trouble and they don't fit in with the accepted norms of classroom behaviour. They can be difficult to like and unpopular with the majority of kids in your class – THAT is their disadvantage.

Some kids are born struggling socially; others have been created by circumstance. These children are socially disabled, and to accept that is crucial. Without this acceptance, empathy won't grow. Without empathy, subjectivity and paranoia flourish. Empathy excels as the curative medicine. By accepting the nature of the disability and treating it as such, teachers are more likely to find responses and attitudes that work. (But it's not easy!)

A teacher's negative experiences with difficult pupils can cloud thinking and the problem then becomes cyclical. Difficult behaviour is then constantly reinforced and just grows. It is not unusual for teachers to view difficult pupils as inevitable, rather than a fresh challenge each morning. These children can be labelled unreachable, incurable, their behaviour unforgivable. From that sort of condemnation, they have no escape.

To search optimistically, to experiment and see the problems as contemporary and not historical is a successful pathway to finding solutions. A positive mindset is difficult and requires clear thinking, not just when dealing with the immediate problem, but before the difficulties arise. That's the purpose of this book – to help you see that these children are reachable, and teachable.

The SEMH pupil's dysfunctionality should not be generalised: each individual SEMH pupil has had a different pathway to his or her desperation. They have few internal pathways to improvement; those pathways have to be discovered by you and strengthened in them.

How to use this book

This book includes quick, easy and practical ideas for you to dip in and out of to support your knowledge and understanding of children with social, emotional and mental health difficulties.

Each idea includes:

- a catchy title, easy to refer to and share with your colleagues
- an interesting quote linked to the idea
- a summary of the idea in bold, making it easy to flick through the book and identify an idea you want to use at a glance
- a step-by-step guide to implementing the idea.

Each idea also includes one or more of the following:

Teaching tip

Practical tips and advice for how and how not to run the activity or put the idea into practice.

Taking it further

Ideas and advice for how to extend the idea or develop it further.

Bonus idea ★

There are 45 bonus ideas in this book that are extra exciting, extra original and extra interesting.

Share how you use these ideas and find out what other practitioners have done using **#100ideas**.

Getting to know
what it's all about

Part 1

What does SEMH mean?

'Children described as SEMH are hugely varied in their presenting behaviours.'

SEMH is a shorthand description of a whole range of challenging behaviours.

Teaching tip

Think about the list detailed in this idea and see how, bit by bit, you can persuade these children to change this alienated view of life.

Many children who come under the heading of SEMH live lives that are cruel, abusive, neglected, rejecting or confusing. Their lives are full of contradictions and paradoxes. When they go home and before they come to school, they learn to survive – some not so well. They try to manage their lives in their own way when they are far too young to make the right judgments.

On a typical day, a typical child with SEMH might come into school, more or less in school uniform, often from a difficult wake up and an eventful breakfast (if any) and perhaps leave for school with little ceremony. Then they meet you! You tell them what they are going to do and quite rightly expect obedience. You care about them, direct them and expect them to learn.

But what do they think about you and other children, with all your demands and rules, and how does this manifest in their behaviour?

- They can feel hostility when you ask them to do things they don't like doing and, in many cases, can't do!
- They may sit with children who behave, enjoy working and get on with the adults.
- They are like fish out of water; they wriggle, bite, jump and can't settle.
- They want to be in their self-determined world, where they can do what they want, in the way they want.
- They feel inferior to the smart children.

- If they see a weakness at home, they exploit it, so they do the same in school.
- They feel their work is inferior to most of the class and that's not fair.
- They experience pain, both emotionally and physically, and think that's how the world works, so why not pass it on.
- They mostly receive little praise for anything.
- They receive lots of negatives from you and the general environment of the school.
- They feel vulnerable in school, because it's not set up for them.
- They are often in trouble for doing things that come naturally: hitting, swearing, running away, throwing things.
- They behave instinctively and 'get done for it'.

It's a long list, and I am sure you could add more. Obviously not every child with SEMH thinks or feels everything on the list but most have elements of the above.

Bonus idea ★

Remember that this section is about the pupils with SEMH and not you; your job is to create an environment that might counteract some of it.

Aliens in your classroom

'These children *want* to be liked and rewarded by you.'

In pupils with SEMH, the ability to adapt is weak and insufficient. Their world outside school is what they regard as normal, and therefore school can seem like another planet.

Pupils' mode of conduct has been modelled long before they come to school. Their adult role models are often dysfunctional and inadequate. Their siblings may share the same attitudes and behaviours. So, the culture of school is alien to them and at times incomprehensible.

But not all is doom and gloom; paradoxically, your behaviour can counteract most of the behaviours listed in Idea 1. Because, deep down, they would like to be just like everybody else in the class – successful! But children with SEMH are burdened by social and academic failure. They do want to shine for you. Hold on to that, because that is the key to counteracting their poor self-image in your school. It can be incredibly rewarding and exciting when it happens.

If you are empathetic to this paradox, your responses will be less confrontational and more therapeutic. This will lessen the child's anxiety and enable you to be more positive in your approach.

Categorising disruption

'It was easier once everyone was on the same page.'

By categorising behaviour in four ways, we can clearly describe and differentiate between levels of seriousness. Ideas 3 to 6 will give you strategies for dealing with each of these levels of behaviour.

The Elton Report was commissioned by the government in 1989 to look into disruption in schools. Although there were serious incidents, they found a plethora of minor behaviours interrupting studies, and the effects on teaching were far greater at the lower end of the scale; generally, little has changed in today's schools. Categorising what behaviours interrupt teaching in your classroom may help to formulate a more comprehensive view of disruptive behaviours. I have listed behaviour in four levels: disruption; serious disruption; behaviours requiring significant intervention; and behaviours requiring teacher intervention to prevent harm.

Level 1 'Disruption' is a low-level disturbance that is irritating and has the potential to escalate.

Level 1 – disruption:

- refusing to sit in identified place
- making inappropriate noise or noises
- not doing as told after a warning
- walking around without permission
- talking while the teacher is talking
- refusing to work or distracting others
- deliberately spoiling the work requested.

These behaviours are irritating and need careful management by an appropriate intervention or they may escalate. Although they appear minor, you need to be careful how you respond. Try to avoid getting into long conversations with children demonstrating Level 1 behaviour.

Teaching tip

Level 1 disruption is a low-level disturbance that is irritating. At Level 1, our SEMH pupils are testing you. They know what they are doing is wrong and may be just wanting to play a game. It takes up time and distracts you from teaching. Unfortunately, these disruptions can easily escalate!

Taking it further

How you describe levels of behaviour in your classroom/school may be different from those in this book, and feel free to develop your own. These four levels are based on their effect on the teacher's ability to teach the whole class.

Bonus idea ★

You can read the full Elton Report online here: http://www.educationengland.org.uk/documents/elton/elton1989.html

More serious incidents

'Level 2 behaviours are a demand for your attention.'

These behaviours challenge your authority and make it significantly harder to teach than is preferable.

Teaching tip

Using this categorisation of behaviours, you will be able to differentiate between levels of disruption and serious disruption. You will have a more objective view of a child's problems and differentiate the strength of intervention required; see Idea 3.

Level 2 – more serious disruption:

- refusing to sit down at all
- continually attempting to disrupt one or more pupils
- shouting out when the teacher is addressing the whole class
- using threatening language towards another pupil or pupils
- deliberately damaging equipment
- swearing loudly for effect
- continually asking silly questions about the work set
- refusing to work.

This set of behaviours is taking it a step further; it is a challenge to your authority and a serious distraction to your teaching. Attention is taken away from the whole class and directed at our children with SEMH. The curtains are open and the child wants to start the play. All the other children are watching you both. Level 1 can usually be resolved with careful management; this is a much bigger challenge, needing all your de-escalation skills. By being seriously disruptive, the child challenges you directly, requiring immediate attention. This prevents whole-class teaching. Now be aware of other less disruptive pupils who may take advantage of your distraction.

When things get hot

'Behaviours in Level 3 may cause teaching to be halted.'

You can't allow Level 3 behaviours to go unchecked. They stop general teaching and require action. Only follow the prescribed procedures.

Level 3 – behaviour requiring significant intervention:

- out of seat with aggressive intent
- threatening another pupil or pupils
- continually shouting out, ignoring the teacher's request to calm down
- running out of the classroom or teaching area
- refusing to line up, disrupting transition
- hurting another pupil
- serious damage to school equipment
- making lewd and suggestive remarks directly at another pupil
- shouting at teacher or another adult
- running around outside the classroom.

A line has been crossed and the pupil is getting out of control. Not just your control, but maybe their own control. These are examples of dangerous and threatening behaviours. The escalation is moving up a sharp incline and if not halted could end badly. The class has lost your attention altogether and teaching has stopped.

Children behave in this threatening way because they are stressed. They may have been stimulated by their immediate surroundings or have unresolved threatening experiences outside school.

IDEA 6

OUT OF CONTROL

'These extreme behaviours can be physically threatening.'

Out-of-control behaviour might require drastic action. You need to identify out-of-control behaviour quickly and know how to respond.

egment
Teaching tip

When faced with out-of-control behaviours, class adults should keep calm and NOT PANIC. Yes, I know it's not easy, but it is a prerequisite if you are to make any sort of successful intervention. See Part 7 for examples of calm interventions. Keep calm, think and act.

Bonus idea ★

Once you have defined the behaviours, you can assign meaningful descriptions to your levels. Give them simple labels such as 'Level 1', 'Level 2', etc. or 'Low severity', 'Medium severity', etc. Each level can contain a different number of categories. A good exercise for the whole school would be to agree on the categories and place children in their appropriate levels. Then every adult would understand the school's definition of disruption.

Level 4 – behaviours requiring teacher intervention to prevent harm:

- assaulting or attempting to assault another pupil
- pushing over furniture likely to cause damage to another pupil or the classroom
- throwing equipment around that is likely to cause harm
- direct assault or threatening assault on a teacher or other adult
- screaming abuse and swearing at a teacher or another adult
- dangerous behaviour requiring restraint.

These behaviours require physical management and assistance for you and perhaps other adults. If you have been trained to use physical prompting, moving the child or physically restraining them, then be prepared. The lesson has gone and the safety of all other children is paramount.

It is essential that you feel confident about:

- Physical prompting – move the child out of the classroom, safely, using an approved hold.
- Physical restraint – being able to hold a child safely using an approved method.

Teachers may dislike or lack confidence when using this method of managing children. If so, either retrain in this area or talk to the SENCO so other arrangements can be made.

Looking at you

Part 2

Enhance your confidence and gain skills

'Every move you make, every word you say, they'll be watching you.'

There are many skills to acquire that will improve your work with SEMH children. Every success enhances your confidence in overcoming difficult behaviours. By establishing a positive cycle, you gain in confidence and, consequently, increase your skill set.

Teaching tip

Try to create a classroom that is both fair and transparent, where difficult behaviour is managed consistently, using clear guidelines that are evenly applied.

Listed below are some characteristics that might describe how you see yourself as a classroom teacher.

1 Be honest, and tick five positives and five negatives.
2 Now think about how most children see you and select five positives and five negatives.
3 Lastly, think carefully about your SEMH pupils and how they think about you.

> quiet, noisy, loud, shy, confident, calm, too silly, good sense of humour, enthusiastic, irritable, lively, sensitive, inconsistent, prone to panic, too serious, boring, understanding, consistent, disaffected, decisive, unconfident, clear, negative, tentative, positive, lively, assertive, supportive, fair, quick to anger, good team player, respectful, nice

What are the differences between 1, 2 and 3? What can you glean from that?

Here are some questions to help you reflect on this exercise:

- Did you find it difficult to restrict yourself to just five positives? If so, add a few more.
- Think carefully about your negatives and ask yourself why you selected those particular characteristics. Are they habitual or do they

come into play when you are tired or under pressure? Think about them, and see how you can present in a different way.

- What five positives and negatives did you choose for how most children might think about you? Were there any differences from your five regarding yourself? Do you sometimes irritate them by your insistence on certain values? Can you appear boring, or even a bit too lively?
- Perhaps most significantly, how do you think your SEMH pupils think about you? Do they think you are a bit negative, get angry too quickly or are inconsistent?

I am not suggesting you can be all things to all pupils but I am asking you to think about it. Pupils with SEMH can find it difficult when you don't react consistently. Perhaps SEMH pupils might think it's not fair when you say to a typical pupil, 'Well Brian, I didn't expect *you* to behave like that' – meaning that SEMH pupils might.

> **Bonus idea** ★
>
> Whenever possible, be positive with your comments, especially with SEMH pupils – they rarely feel the warm rays of the sun in school! Don't forget, working with these pupils requires resilience.

How empathetic are you?

'Empathy is not always easy to summon up.'

Children with social, emotional and mental health difficulties are not simply 'naughty'; they actually have a disability. Without accepting that premise, empathy will be difficult to develop.

If you just see children with SEMH as destroyers, you are in for a very unhappy teaching career. They will always be in your classroom, so let's create a better perception of them. By doing so you will feel more able to help and actually begin to like them more! Below are a few points you might like to mull over.

- Children with SEMH have all the same needs and wishes as any other pupil but they're mixed up with learnt behaviour long before they crash into the required discipline of school.
- They can challenge all aspects of your management skills, but deep inside they want YOU to win, because that gives them security.
- They want you to recognise their skills. They have them, but they are well hidden under a mountain of insecurity.
- They want to be part of the group but it's difficult for them to find the right friends.
- They would love to laugh with others, but only manage to scorn alone.
- They want to make a good start to the day but tend to find the initial hour or so too challenging, and start off on the wrong foot.
- They feel threatened if their flawed behaviour is exposed to the class or even to a small group of their peers.

Start and finish with a smile

'There are not many certainties when dealing with children with SEMH, but this is one.'

Lots of smiles and positives at the beginning of a lesson make the odd correction more bearable for pupils with SEMH.

For most SEMH pupils, school has always been a big problem; they find the rules difficult, group membership a problem, child-to-adult communication too complicated and your authority problematic. First thing in the morning, they can hit school carrying all sorts of anxieties, which may not be immediately apparent. They may be cold or wet and are often tired, so to be met with a smile and a special hello is a good start. Perhaps just a touch on the shoulder can be reassuring. Don't ask too much about how they are feeling – that could cause ripples.

Smile at each child as they come in and see what you get back; keep that information in the bank for later. The more information you get at the beginning of the day, the more data you have for later, when life might be more interesting and difficult.

Think about variable tones of voice and appropriate vocabulary to encourage listening, and, above all, be enthusiastic about the content. Keep your introduction reasonably short; I have observed 20-minute introductions, which could have tempted me to be disruptive. Once the introduction has been completed, stay close to the SEMH pupils, making sure they understand what is required. Prompt positively, e.g. 'What a good start', 'Well done', 'I like that'. The transition from introduction to starting work is a danger time; watch out and monitor!

Taking it further

The start of the day is crucial: it has to be bright, interesting and easily understood by all the pupils. No ambiguities, no boring diatribe but sparkling and interesting, with the odd funny joke. A bit of well-managed child participation goes down well.

Bonus idea ★

To allay children's initial fears, your introduction should be easy to understand, without ambiguity: simple, clear and exciting. Any reading material should be as easy as possible. Your handwriting on the whiteboard should be well formed and easy to read, a simple script. Multi-media presentations can stimulate and prevent early frustration.

Ask these questions

'Can you manage serious incidents with confidence?'

Dealing with children with SEMH is complicated because you are dealing with chaotic, challenging and sometimes dangerous pupils with paradoxical behaviour.

When working at the crisis stage, the questions you have to ask are:

- Do you have a strong enough will and desire to win over the most difficult and demanding pupils?
- Do you have sufficient knowledge and experience of working with pupils at this hard end of the market?
- Do you need training in the management of these extreme behaviours?
- Is the quality of the call-out/back-up support you receive from the school adequate?
- Are the extremes of behaviour you are expected to work with containable?
- Is the general level of discipline in the school good enough to support a calm classroom?
- Is the quality of support services in the school, including the senior leadership team (SLT), SENCO and important external services, adequate?
- And perhaps most important of all: do you have any empathy for these children?

Your ability to be an effective teacher and cope with challenging pupils included in your class is also dependent on the ability of the school to support you appropriately. Don't be afraid to request more support, training and effective back-up.

Bonus idea ★

Work hard, be diligent and keep clear, up-to-date records of all incidents, including the school's participation in major challenges.

Getting a lesson going

'It's like setting a trap – catching the achievement and showing it off. The more of that the better!'

Producing differentiated material can be hard work for you but can prevent a sense of hopelessness. Tailor activities to different skills and abilities, making sure one or two of them match the SEMH pupils' individual learning styles. Give them a chance to shine.

The best start to the day would be for children with SEMH to complete a lesson with no incidents and with learning targets achieved.

1 Carefully plan your introduction; not too long and as interesting as possible – a bit like a film trailer!
2 Start the day with simple tasks; don't go straight into English or maths, as these are contentious areas for SEMH pupils.
3 After your introduction, make a seamless move to work. Transition is a danger period; try to reduce classroom mobility, add lots of positives and keep smiling.
4 Any materials required should be easy to distribute with little mobility.
5 Keep the interest going by constant positive remarks, made as close as possible to the pupil to aid concentration.
6 Finish with a quiet fanfare wherever possible.
7 Be wary of problems at the end of a phase; keep the class calm before the transition to the next phase. (After success, monitor transition; positives can go to their heads.)

Keep prompting the class by signalling what is expected. Make positive comments, especially physically close to SEMH children. Think about the pace at which you move the class on. Have intervals in which you share aspects of the learning target.

Teaching tip

Getting a lesson going and keeping the momentum at a manageable pace can make all the difference. Try not to leave SEMH pupils behind; it can leave them with a sense of hopelessness. They want to feel included and be part of the flow.

Bonus idea ★

Preparation is key. Don't slip out of the classroom for forgotten items, and have spare equipment for those who have forgotten theirs. Don't ask SEMH children to share books or equipment: they generally can't share. Keep your lesson watertight, and have an option ready if things don't work out.

Presenting yourself to the class

'Come on: standing up straight, shoulders back and a good clear voice gets things off on the right foot.'

From the very beginning of the day, you are watched by the children with SEMH. How you stand, move around and talk can be a guide to how you are feeling. If you present as a wilted flower at the beginning of the day, the next five or so hours are going to be, let's say, difficult.

How you present yourself at school is the 'you' as seen by your pupils. Look at yourself in the mirror just before you go to school and ask yourself two basic questions:

- How do the children see me?
- How do I want the children to see me?

Does it matter? Well, yes it does! Are you happy with your appearance? Do you look strong and interesting? Do you look confident? Being presentable is part of the job; how you dress and even smell provide an important guide to how you are feeling. Some mornings are more difficult than others, but the children see you as special for them – even our SEMH pupils, oh yes, they do. Don't underestimate how important you are to them.

You are an actor on stage, closely watched by a discerning audience. To help you present well, stand upright with a straight back, head up and shoulders relaxed, ready to start the day. Move around with a confident step at the appropriate speed, avoiding jerky moves. Speak calmly in welcoming, gentle tones with lots of praise. Do not give too much direction; you might feel like raising your voice but try hard not to.

What's your style and does it work?

'You can't start the lesson well without first planning well.'

Starting well is essential (see Idea 9), but pre-planning is *critical*. Don't just plan what you are going to teach but plan the style of your teaching too, including grouping and layout.

There are a number of things to consider when planning lessons, in addition to the lesson itself. Think about how you group the pupils: small groups, single working, splitting the class into large working groups, explorative or directional, practical groups or more academic subsets? Whatever the groupings, think about the behavioural consequences. Once a particular style of teaching is decided upon, you have to pre-empt what might happen.

Classroom geography has to be taken into consideration too. How do you set up work bases? Here are some things to consider.

- Are all tables facing the front, two on a table? This can work with a new, difficult class.
- Could you have four or even six children round a table, all facing inward? This might be too many distractions for SEMH children.
- Do you have a seating plan or do pupils sit where they like? Free will is fine but does it *work* in your classroom?
- Bright pupils on one table, the SEMH children on a special table, with more staff? Socially challenged all on the same table?
- Do you have a mobility plan or can pupils move about when and where they like? Free mobility might overwhelm SEMH children with too many opportunities.
- Do you have a desk at the front or do you work from different parts of the room?

Teaching tip

During your lesson-planning, consider the way you organise your class, the sequence of lessons, integrated learning and reward systems. Also think about how you deliver and manage learning targets and how you manage change from one phase to another.

Taking it further

If a particular classroom layout works for you then that's okay but don't be dogmatic about it. Experiment, try different ways of organising your classroom. Most of all, don't be afraid to change. But don't forget SEMH pupils and how change might affect them!

Be creative

'A good learning experience for children with SEMH can make the next one appear that little bit more appealing.'

When planning the whole day, consider different ways of teaching. Using the same method throughout the day might even turn a 'regular' child into a disruptive one. A variety of styles might help you to enjoy your teaching more.

Preparation
All teaching is challenging, but the more creative your preparation and the more you put into it, the more likely you are to have a good day. One good day can make the next day easier to teach.

Structure
Try to arrange your subjects so that more challenging areas don't follow on from each other. If SEMH pupils experience consecutive areas of difficulty, like English followed by maths, the learning tension can grow very significantly! Above all, experiment. Don't just teach the same way all the time and expect it to work; you and the children might get bored – especially SEMH pupils. Surprise them but prepare well for any changes; it can be difficult but, properly managed, can be a game-changer.

Timing
Lesson timing is about the pace you teach at and the way in which you maintain interest and attention in your lessons. The conventional format of an introduction, followed by work, closing books and leaving the classroom is not an effective model for any child, especially those with SEMH. Plan your lessons to have changes in pace and attention span.

Does your classroom work?

Part 3

Starting the day

'Always remember school is a pupil's home for the day, a place where they might be able to settle and succeed.'

Creating a secure start to the day can help pupils settle and recognise that school is a safe space.

The children we have to take special care with can come from a variety of home settings – from the chaotic/abusive to the obsessively well organised. When they reach the school, what kind of environment do they enter? Some come to school very early, while others might need a bit of nudging before they will enter your classroom. What do they see? Firstly, they check you out and then maybe head for their desk. How does the day start for them? A drawing, reading book or a chat, or is there a selection of starters to choose from?

Reflect on the beginning of your school day and ask yourself:

- Is there a clear routine for bags, lunchboxes and coats? Does it work?
- Can pupils move around or do they have to stay in their seats?
- Can they natter in activity areas?
- Can they sit on the carpet near your desk?
- Do you make time for a little chat?

When a pupil with SEMH enters the classroom, take a good look at the expression on their face. Can you see anxiety, sadness or even anger? If you're concerned then stay close, have a brief chat and make a special effort to find something interesting for them to do near you. Most of all, listen carefully to what they say and measure the emotion in their response. Be low key but try to keep as near as possible to your starter routine. An early bubble is very difficult to manage, as it can disrupt the rest of the day.

If a child is disturbed at the beginning of the day:

- Don't let the child get too far away from an adult.
- Don't ask direct questions about feelings; just wait and listen.
- Don't get too pushy about work, but expect something.
- Keep the pupil away from the children they dislike.

These 'dos and don'ts' are hugely important for SEMH pupils. Consistency is essential at the start of the day, with clear expectations. Gently persuade and encourage them to do the right thing. Remember that pupils can sometimes arrive at school after quite challenging starts to the day at home.

> **Bonus idea** ★
>
> If you can sense a difficult start to the day for a pupil with SEMH, perhaps get your TA to take them out of the classroom to do a little 'job' for a few minutes.

Do you have a seating plan?

'The single most important thing about your classroom is that it is yours. It's your territory; it's YOUR home for the day.'

Seating plans state clearly where you want all pupils to sit. It's your classroom and that is how you want to organise it.

What does a seating plan signal to all pupils and especially to SEMH pupils? It says clearly and without ambiguity that the classroom is managed by you for the purpose of education and learning. Who sits where and with whom is your decision and is a manifestation of your authority. That might sound a bit high and mighty but it is required for the safety of all and the smooth delivery of the curriculum.

Where do you want pupils to sit and why? That is the essential question you need to answer.

1 Do you want to sit all the 'regular' pupils together or do you want a mix of children at each table?
2 Do you want the SEMH pupils spread around the class?
3 Do you want all SEMH children together, with lots of support?
4 Do you want the SEMH pupils next to you?
5 Do you change seating plans for different subjects?
6 Should our SEMH pupils be near the front?
7 Should they be seated away from their friends?
8 Should there be distance between them and the next table, for easy access?
9 Should they be on the side of the table that faces you, so you have easy eye contact?
10 Should they be away from the doors?

Think carefully about these questions and come to your own conclusions – it depends on how you teach.

Scanning the class

'Keep your eyes moving across the whole class, stopping here and there.'

Simply by regular scanning, you can reduce triggers and prevent the development of unwanted and disruptive behaviours.

In your classroom, SEMH pupils look for those little areas where you can't see them. You should have a clear view of every child in your classroom – no screens, cupboards or large objects to hide behind. Even 'regular' children and those just on the margin can mess around in a blind spot.

Scanning is a tool that keeps everybody safe. It's not complicated. It is simply running your eyes constantly over the whole class. Wherever you are in the classroom, gym, art room, hall or playground, every 20 seconds or so check what all the pupils are doing. This simple, easy process can prevent the escalation of serious behaviours.

- Some pupils respond by feeling secure and therefore staying calm.
- Others see that trying it on is not going to be successful.

You might ask how can I scan when I am working one-to-one or teaching a subset of the class? Well, it's a bit like being in a submarine without a periscope; you have to listen to the sounds around you using auditory scanning. Classes on task have a distinct sound – they can be a bit noisy but there is a nice hum about it. BUT other sounds can creep in, e.g. over-the-top laughter, sharp angry words, chairs being pushed, an object slammed on a desk. Possibly the most worrying is when the whole class goes quiet. Whoops – something's wrong.

Teaching tip

Just remember, scanning plus eye contact can prevent the growth of disruption. Catching that first odd or unusual sound can prevent an escalation which could flower into something problematic. It can be quite tiring, but when the class – and especially our SEMH pupils – learn that your eyes and ears are on the ball, they are less likely to cause trouble!

Taking it further

As you scan, you can often make eye contact, because SEMH pupils will also be watching you. This is a great opportunity. You can smile, nod, even wink if things look good, or frown or shake your head if things look dodgy. No words spoken, no confrontation – success!

Understanding pupils' social groupings

'Every class has its own unique pattern of social relationships: popular pupils, unpopular pupils, social isolates.'

Most pupils form cohesive and positive subgroups. Dysfunctional pupils form dysfunctional subgroups and create major problems for you and the class. Use sociometry to analyse social groupings, then use this information to your advantage.

Teaching tip

The outcomes listed here are common to the hundreds of sociometric analyses I have undertaken in both primary and secondary schools.

Every class has a network of complex social groupings. Every class is unique in its patterns of relationships. Socially, boys and girls tend to have separate styles of relating to each other. In most classes, boys and girls have distinctly different bondings. At primary and early secondary level, mixed-gender social groups are rare.

Over many years, I have used a technique called sociometry, a quantitative method for measuring social relationships with Year 2 upwards. It works by simply asking every child in the class two questions:

- Which three children would you like to sit next to? (like)
- Which three children don't you want to sit next to? (dislike)

The question should be about a normal class environment. Questions such as 'who do you like and don't like?' are too emotive. The answers should then be placed on a graph in the form of a matrix, matching likes and dislikes and totalling likes and dislikes.

Consistent outcomes are as follows:

- Girls are generally more popular than boys and boys are more disliked than girls.
- Girls form strong mutual 'like groups' and boys' groupings are more fragmented.

- Some pupils are neither liked nor disliked; these can be either boys or girls.
- Girls' mutual 'like groups' tend to be the centre of a network of positive relationships.
- Boys can form some mutual 'like groups' but they are not as prevalent and are more fragmented than girls.
- 'Disliked' boys form disruptive and constantly changing subgroups.
- Mutual dislikes are mainly boys disliking other boys.
- Some boys do choose girls to sit next to, but girls rarely choose boys.
- The majority of significant dislikes are for boys, chosen by both boys and girls.

Here is an example of how you can use this information to gain a greater insight into your pupils and their relationships.

Case study

Here are the results of a study with three different groups. ML indicates 'mutual like' and MD indicates 'mutual dislike'.

Group 1

	A	B	C	D
A		ML	ML	ML
B	ML		ML	ML
C	ML	ML		ML
D	ML	ML	ML	

Group 2

	A	B	C	D
A		ML	ML	
B	ML		ML	ML
C	ML	ML		
D		ML		

Group 3

	A	B	C	D
A		ML	ML	
B	ML		MD	
C				
D		MD	ML	

The pupils in Group 1 mutually choose each other and form a tight positive group at the centre of the class's social structure. This central group is usually all girls but can be boys. Group 2 is an example of a less closely-knit group. There are some mutual likes but the group is not as tightly-knit as Group 1. Group 3 is an example of a dysfunctional subgroup – usually boys – containing SEMH pupils. Group 3 is a group that rarely stays constant and is full of social strife, preventing harmony in the group and causing chaos for the class and the teacher.

Bonus idea ★

To obtain genuine responses, a teacher or TA should ask the questions away from the group, with an assurance that these answers are confidential.

Group dynamics

'SEMH children often have poor social skills and consequently are not able to integrate into the positive social structures of the class.'

SEMH pupils often don't form friendship groups in the classroom because they find maintaining relationships difficult. Children who are not chosen by any pupil are isolated, but a simple change to your classroom layout can help improve their integration.

What does a sociometric analysis mean for you as a class teacher regarding children with SEMH?

- Most children don't interact with SEMH pupils socially and avoid contact.
- SEMH pupils select 'fringe' children with whom they form irregular and sometimes volatile subgroups.

The dynamics of SEMH subgroups can cause significant disruption within the classroom. The boys in these groups can be best of friends one minute and enemies the next. They are, in a sense, trapped by their own social inadequacies and don't have the skills to break out. These negative subgroups can be occasionally joined by marginal children who sometimes like 'having a laugh'!

There are numerous problems that can be caused by negative subgroups of SEMH pupils:

- They want to sit with their mates, but relationships are not consistent, consequently causing behaviour problems for the class and you.
- As many children find them difficult, they are not successful in group activities; they roam the classroom, constantly out of their seat!
- They want to sit next to pupils they can control and use them to support disruption.

- They ARE aware of the animosity of the rest of the class and can call out to attract attention, especially when supported by a negative subgroup.

Think about using a 'circle of friends' – a tried-and-tested technique. Often, SEMH pupils' dysfunctional behaviour arises from isolation and a sense of hopelessness. Design a space around the difficult pupil (this could be part of a seating plan) and fill it with understanding and positive children. Coach their peers to respond positively. Ask them to praise good behaviour and work, laugh at their jokes and do not appear threatened by the maladjusted behaviour. If you get the 'circle of friends' chemistry right, it can deliver major rewards for you, the class and, most importantly, the children with SEMH.

Bonus idea

Wherever possible, keep the individual members of negative subgroups away from each other in class, the dining room, line-ups and activities. This will help overall behaviour.

IDEA 20

Lining up

'Lining up is the beginning of a new activity, not separate from it.'

Transition times, such as at the end of a lesson, are crucial times for SEMH pupils. Good lining-up practices can ease these transitions.

Teaching tip

A well-behaved line is a strong and effective way of managing the whole class. It sends out a clear statement to all concerned.

Taking it further

Lining up gives a clear message to the class, setting the tone for what comes next. If the next phase starts with disorder, it's difficult to recover. End a phase in disorder and it becomes difficult to start the next one in control. If things do go wrong, sit everybody down, state your requirements and start again. Be consistent about the behaviour you require before moving on to the next phase. The class will get tired of the process and SEMH pupils will eventually get the message. Never lower the standard of behaviour required.

Children are asked to line up at various times of the day: first thing, before leaving or entering the classroom, in the playground, queuing for lunch and many more. All these times relate to beginning or ending a phase of the school day. This is a crucial time for SEMH pupils; it involves movement and order. They are not always at their best at these times and require some shepherding. Here are a few questions you might like to ask yourself:

- Do you have a line order? If not, try it out; you might be surprised at the difference it makes.
- Do you talk to the class about line order and ask for suggestions? Tell them why class order is good for the class and state clearly why it is required.
- Where do you place SEMH pupils in the line: front, back or spread out along the line? Keep them away from their subgroup to prevent disruption and negative interactions.
- Do you send children with SEMH to the back? It's not always a good idea – it can cause even greater problems. Place them next to a class adult and keep a close eye on them.
- Do you keep the line waiting until all is still, eyes on you? If not, you move to the next period of the day with inadequate control.
- Where do you place yourself in the line? Near the front to control the pace of movement can work well.

These choices reflect your individual style, but do keep them consistent!

Quality provision

'It is all about being smart in every area of your professional conduct.'

This book is about managing SEMH pupils; the comments I make about classrooms and your style of teaching are targeted at coping with that significant element. How you present to the class and specifically to children with SEMH is critical.

What you are like outside school may be different from the person you need to project as a professional teacher. What your kitchen at home looks like is up to you, but your classroom has to look good and be fit for purpose.

SEMH pupils often have little mercy: they spot weakness and exploit it. If your management is a problem and your classroom is confusing, you might need to think hard about changes.

- Perhaps you could change where you teach from or move around more.
- Think about consistency regarding rules and expectations.
- Could you reorganise your classroom, making it more fit for purpose?
- Do you need to be more inventive with the materials you use, improve the wall displays or jazz them up a bit?

Teaching styles can often vary, from the authoritarian to the more liberal professionals, with a whole range of options in between – and they can all work. Because SEMH pupils test us to the limit, we have to be sure our classrooms are functional, workable and consistent. Don't be lazy about your classroom; any damage to displays has to be made good immediately. Damaged furniture has to be replaced straightaway.

Does all this sound picky? Well, it's meant to, because all these little things make up the total picture of your classroom.

Scanning to prevent disruption

'Scanning is a bit like checking on the speed of your car, making sure you don't go too fast and maybe hurt someone.'

Using scanning as a preparation for action can save so much pain and suffering.

Challenging children tend to gradually build up their behaviour by responding to triggers and certain types of stimulation. If you have been scanning consistently, you will be aware of the build-up and be more able to deal with the behaviour in a proactive way. As you have watched both the birth and the development of the behaviour, you will be better equipped if an intervention is required.

Get close to the theatre of action – use your teaching position in the class to reduce tension. Every move, action or instruction you make that is related to the increased heat should be monitored by further purposeful scanning. Make it perfectly clear that you are observing the child and the behaviour.

- Don't turn your back on the situation but be constantly vigilant.
- If the heat does not reduce but stays about the same, keep watching; avoid long periods of eye contact but increase the frequency.
- A single word or even a facial expression can keep the temperature at a steady but not critical heat.
- Be on top of the situation: keep up the observation. If the problem reduces, withdraw gradually and increase the scanning interval.

Teaching assistants

Part 4

Choosing TAs

'If a new TA is to be appointed to work in your classroom, you should lobby the SLT regarding the ability and personality required.'

Remember, a TA should be a supportive adult who will need to be sympathetic to your management methods. If possible, you could sit in on the appointment interview. If not, talk to the SLT about the kind of professional required as a support in your classroom with your children.

Schools can vary in the amount of investment they make in support staff. Pupil premium can provide funds to invest and school may be funded with regard to SEN children.

TAs are a mixed group of adults, who often tend to be women, and the majority tend to be parents, who may have children in the school. In many cases they have no specific training for the job. Often, however, they can be given difficult tasks to perform, including specific responsibilities for extremely difficult children. In some cases that means that the **least** trained staff have the **most** difficult tasks.

It is important to appoint the right people in the position of TA. Selection might be made easier if the job advertised has specific requirements and identifies responsibilities. Here are some questions to consider in your context:

- What kind of TAs do you have in your school?
- Do you have any higher-level TAs?
- Do you have a lead TA?
- Do you have TAs trained for academic support?
- Do you have TAs specifically for nurturing?
- Do senior TAs have a management role?
- Are TAs represented on the SLT?

The status of TAs

'TAs should be directed by you. You have to be clear about what you want.'

TAs, when guided and properly trained, can be of immense value to the child, class and school.

In the majority of schools, TAs are a separate entity and not significantly included in the central hub of the school. Yet in many cases they are close to the most significant problems a school has. These valuable members of staff can often be sidelined when discussing significant behavioural and academic problems. This may be an opportunity lost. So, what can be done?

- The school could establish a hierarchy of TAs, which gives responsibility to, say, a lead TA or perhaps a higher-level TA. This could enable good communication between the TAs and the SLT.
- An audit of TAs' skills and abilities could be undertaken, so that the right staff can be chosen for a specific task.
- Staff chosen to work with SEMH pupils should be given specific training in relation to the disability.
- TAs could be coached by either the class teacher or perhaps the SENCO in relation to the specific therapies the school prefers.

This increased support would change the way in which a TA might deal with a child. It also increases the skill level to that required to manage the most difficult children and gives the TAs an increased level of respect. When a TA does get closer to a child and a positive relationship is formed, the effect on the child, the class and the school can be very significant.

Teaching tip

Nurture your TA, include them in your planning and give them the status they deserve. TAs, just like teachers, can have children in the school, and this can cause problems. This dynamic has been reported to me by many teachers and senior staff. This is a difficult issue, but has to be faced openly.

Managing TAs in the classroom

'Get to know your TA, but remember you're the boss.'

Both teachers and TAs have strengths and weaknesses but it is the teacher's job to direct the working practice of the TA. That is not an easy job because there is often a discrepancy in educational background and training. However, such differences do not mean a discrepancy in the ability to nurture.

I have observed in classrooms and elsewhere in schools the varied relationships between teachers and TAs. It varies enormously from rewarding to acceptance, with some tinges of disdain and all that comes between.

Matching a teacher with a TA is a skill that requires understanding the nature of both individuals and their capacity to complement each other – a bit like a marriage. It is crucial therefore that there are frank discussions between teacher and TA about the basic protocols and working practices of the classroom. Some TAs are appointed to manage SEMH pupils; others are deployed according to the needs of the whole class. When a TA is asked to work with a SEMH child, you must be clear about what is expected. At a minimum, the TA will need the following information:

- the pupil's behaviour patterns
- identified difficult periods of the day
- the academic abilities of the SEMH child
- a variety of responses that might be required
- appropriate language to be used when things get difficult
- appropriate actions to be taken if things become too problematic to manage
- a flexible timetable for the TA to follow
- a need for a discussion regarding behaviour at the end of each day.

Teaching tip

Don't just say, 'Here is the child, keep him quiet.' Like most expedient practices, sooner or later they just don't work. Be clear between you and the TA what you expect; learn together what works and what doesn't. Only through your sound, unambiguous relationship will the child receive good enough care and education.

Bonus idea ★

SEMH children are sensitive, especially to relationships between adults. It is therefore particularly important that the teacher's working relationship with the TA remains harmonious.

One-to-one communication

'When a TA is given the responsibility of working one-to-one with a child, it is your responsibility to train and guide the TA.'

The language of a SEMH pupil has not always developed at the same rate as their peers. Articulation, too, is not always clear, and consequently misunderstandings can occur. Use these strategies to make communication easier.

Here are a few examples of the advice I would give as a class teacher to a TA:

- When you get into conversation with SEMH pupils, listen closely and resist taking the lead. Don't interject but be prepared to prompt when the conversation breaks down. Resist asking 'What do you mean?' or 'Why?'. Rephrase what you think they might have said when they get tongue-tied.
- Use humour sensitively to repair misunderstandings. SEMH pupils are generally unsuccessful in their communication with most adults. The pupil will feel rewarded by your close attention to what they are saying and how they are saying it.
- Listen with intensity and respect. Let the child feel that they have your complete attention and that you are fascinated by what they are saying.
- When talking one-to-one after an incident, try not to use the word 'why', e.g. 'Why did that happen?', 'Why did you do that?'. Just describe what happened and wait for a response. This approach requires patience and occasionally coping with silence while waiting for a response. This makes for open-ended conversations, which are more likely to be fruitful in the long run and create better understanding.

Working one-to-one with SEMH pupils

'I don't care what she does, just keep her quiet.'

Work closely with your TA and keep an eye on the progress the child is making. If working one-to-one is not successful, change the tactics and try again.

As you may know, there are several ways of working one-to-one with our SEMH pupils. However you go about it, the main aim should be to improve a child's behaviour and attitude to school. However, setting up a one-to-one has to be carefully thought about before beginning such a process.

TAs are often used to settle SEMH pupils in the classroom. They can sit next to a pupil in the classroom all day or just for certain subjects. They can help at lunchtimes or on school outings to prevent inappropriate behaviour. These one-to-ones don't always run smoothly as the purpose can be ill-defined or even repressive.

'I don't care what you do, just keep the kid quiet' – have you heard that from other teachers in your school? Such criteria often end in disaster, and the child might be blamed. If you are going to use one-to-one in the classroom, it has to have a positive purpose. What happens in your classroom is your responsibility. The TA is dealing with your pupil and you have to make clear what kind of work you want them to undertake. That's what you are paid to do and what the TA is paid to do. I know it's not easy, but if you both get it right, then that is a fantastic bonus for the child, the TA and you. This might sound a bit authoritarian but the clearer the line management, the more secure the workplace.

There are a number of questions to consider when thinking about one-to-one work with a TA:

- Does the adult get on with the child in need?
- How does the TA relate to the child in the classroom?
- What understanding does the adult have of the child's difficulties?
- What are the adult's tolerance levels for difficult behaviour generally?
- Has the expected way of working been clearly defined?

You have to analyse what you would like to achieve with a one-to-one resource. Discuss with the child, adult, SENCO and perhaps the parent what is expected.

Working one-to-one outside the classroom

'This is valuable and expensive work; don't waste it.'

Working outside the classroom can sometimes be necessary to ensure children can access the curriculum without distraction. Using play as a reward for completing work outside the classroom can be rewarding for pupils and help the child to build a secure and safe relationship with an adult.

Make sure the child is clear about why they are working outside the classroom. Perhaps suggest an achievable target for the TA and the child to attain. Between them, they could organise an individual reward plan that would need to reflect classroom rewards. Encourage both the child and the adult to own what they are doing. Most of all, don't allow it to drift; keep it alive and on task. If it's not working well, change it before it splits apart. SEMH children experience many breakdowns in relationships, so one in school would not be helpful.

If managed and designed correctly, one-to-one outside the classroom can be hugely successful. Again, it needs clear and well-thought-out planning.

- Due consideration should be given to the age of the child.
- Who is best suited to support the child?
- What time of day should a one-to-one session take place?
- How long should the session last?
- Where should it take place?
- Are there any basic health and safety issues that need to be addressed?

Younger children can vary in their ability to verbalise difficulties. Plan any one-to-one sessions so there is a work period followed by playing time if the work is completed. The aids I would suggest could include snap cards, simple games, a doll's house, family dolls, soft toys, toy cars and perhaps a mat showing a street, park or the inside of a house.

Following the successful completion of the work set, the adult involved should not lead but be prepared to be guided in the child's play. Don't direct; let the child choose and follow their interests. If the child wants the adult to play a part, then care must be taken to follow what the child suggests, *within reason*. For younger pupils, I would suggest that the session should last no more than 30 minutes.

The TA must be supported and a debrief of the session shared with the teacher or SENCO, either immediately after the session or at the end of the day.

> **Bonus idea** ★
>
> These short sessions can be daily or at times in the school day that the child finds particularly difficult. I would recommend that a programme of playing time be designed only after the first three sessions.

One-to-one behaviour reviews

'One-to-one should not be seen as punishment or to "get 'em out of the classroom for a bit". Because if it is, **IT WILL NOT WORK**!'

A regular one-to-one session to review behaviour can have a significant positive impact on behaviour. The one-to-one review is dependent on the adult's skills and the child's needs — somewhere between counselling and coaching.

Teaching tip

Adults in school might all seem like enemies to SEMH children, so an adult listener might be a relief. It gives the child a foothold in the school. Good relationships formed in these one-to-ones can reduce problem behaviours.

With older SEMH pupils, their physical size and general conduct can present acute problems in the classroom. One-to-one sessions shouldn't be used simply to get the child out of the classroom; a connection needs to be made between the behaviour displayed and the content of the one-to-one experience.

Before a one-to-one behaviour review is scheduled, the class teacher, SENCO and TA should identify the specific problems the child creates for the school. A one-to-one for these children requires a significant amount of planning. It's important to ensure a good match between child and adult. There are some staff that enjoy the challenge of working with SEMH children.

A regular one-hour session two or three times a week on set days works well. Sessions can take place at lunchtime or towards the end of the day.

Before the session with the child, make sure all information regarding disruptive behaviour is available, plus any positive remarks. This must not be a telling off session — instead, it should be more like an enquiry into the behaviours. The adult should try not to lead but instead follow the child's view of what happened and encourage clear reporting. That does not mean that the behaviour can't be criticised. Any good reports ought to be positively discussed and, where appropriate, praised.

The benefit for SEMH children when implementing a regular one-to-one behaviour review session is that they are listened to in a calm and non-judgmental way. This may seem like a mild response to quite damaging behaviours. But, by just listening, the adult can give the child a chance to offload, and much can be gained in the interaction.

Taking it further

Sessions on Tuesdays and Fridays generally work well. Tuesday sessions should concentrate on the start of the week, while Fridays offer a chance for a review of the whole week.

Working one-to-one with older children

'One-to-one working should be viewed as a valuable communication opportunity.'

When handled well, one-to-one sessions can calm the child and help them to experience periods in school that are therapeutic and behaviour-changing.

Taking it further

The adult involved, when the time is right, can begin to talk about behaviour generally. Don't rush into it; wait for the right time.

Bonus idea ★

After set work has been completed, perhaps try a short period of story-writing (written by the adult or the child), which gives the child time to natter without direct eye contact. Other options could include competitive games like draughts or snakes and ladders, which create verbal interchange and negotiation. It's better to give the child a selection and let them choose, but don't overwhelm them with too many choices!

With slightly older children, if handled carefully, one-to-one meetings allow the child to:

- develop a safe relationship with a single adult
- verbalise their experiences
- experience calm, non-challenging periods in school
- through play, act out difficult encounters elsewhere.

The first three one-to-one sessions should be reviewed and discussed before designing any future one-to-one sessions. Recordings or notes should be made of each session and discussed with a senior colleague. As these one-to-ones are expensive, the SENCO ought to be kept informed of the content and perhaps any improvement or deterioration in the SEMH pupil's behaviour. The sessions can be daily or take place when SEMH pupils usually experience difficulties in the classroom. This can pre-empt problematic behaviours and keep the child calm. Work can be taken into the session and interspersed with other activities. Primary verbal rewards, like 'well done', 'brilliant' or 'I like that', can be given, or secondary rewards, such as a points system or smiling faces as cumulative rewards, can be successful.

You may be surprised at how effective these short intervals of time can be.

Work outside the classroom

Part 5

Meeting the parents or carers

'Perhaps the most important intervention you can make for our SEMH pupils is a meeting with their parents.'

Remember, SEMH children have normally spent their entire early years with their parents. Children spend far more time with their parents than they do with you. This means that parents have far more influence on behaviour than you do.

A large percentage of children with SEMH do still live with either a parent or a relative, so I will refer to all carers as 'parents'.

Parents vary in their own experience of schooling, parenting and lifestyle. They can be aggressive, depressed, 'normal', nice, submissive, arrogant and all of those. They may already have had several meetings with headteachers, teachers or social workers. Be mindful that their child may have been excluded or moved from a previous school, so inviting them in can bring back bad memories.

Parents may have contradictory ways of resolving difficult behaviour to those used by the school. They don't have your backup systems, advice and skills. When asked to come into school, it could be just one of the many threatening events in their lives. Telling the truth is not always a feature of how they present; that might be too difficult. Their primary loyalty is not to the school but to a complex network of conflicting relationships. Parents' understanding of relationship and loyalty might not be the same as yours. Parents may come together or separately, or with a relative such as a grandparent. In my experience, who attends these meeting may be a clue to the relationship between the primary carers. The absence of significant members of the family may suggest a resistance to engage with the school.

Education, health and care plans

'It is *essential* that parents take part in these meetings. Some parents can be very reluctant to attend.'

An education, health and care plan (EHCP) is a vital tool to help you support a child with SEMH. Meetings about the plan with parents and other external agencies are crucial to make sure everything is on track.

When drawing up the EHCP, and before any meeting, care must be taken to ensure that all data the school has about the child is available for the meeting. You need to draw up a clear picture of the child in school, including dates, events and details of any incidents that may have happened recently. It is essential that all your data relating to behaviour is correct, with clear documentation. You should also bring to the meeting an educational profile of the child and the completed EHCP or examples of the process so far.

If any external professionals are invited, make sure that they are aware of how crucial the meeting is for all concerned and ask them to be punctual. Being late for the meeting is unhelpful and unprofessional. All of this might seem a bit like overkill, but it's not; you are dealing with a very complex case, which has to be dealt with objectively and professionally.

Teaching tip

Do not rely on your own recall of the pupil's behaviour; it may be too subjective. Develop a recording method that is systematic, organised, clear and dated. It could be a diary, signed by you and the pupil at the end of each day, and perhaps reviewed at the end of each week. There are many methods you might already be using but just make sure your data is easy to understand and can be authenticated.

Running an EHCP meeting

'Coming out of the end of the meeting as partners is the ultimate aim.'

During an EHCP meeting, it's vital to keep things on track and moving forward.

Teaching tip

For an EHCP meeting to be really therapeutic, it should end in a good atmosphere of mutual respect. I am aware that it might not be easy, but it is essential.

- Review the details of the plan but make sure there is an adequate amount of time left to discuss how things might change in the future. Too often, the future is given only a little time towards the end of the meeting, but looking forward can be as important as being reflective.
- Clear procedures should be followed and a school secretary should take detailed minutes so that everyone else has just one job – to contribute to the meeting.
- Parents should be made welcome and treated with respect; past conflicts should be disregarded, even though that's not always easy to do.
- The meeting should start on time and, wherever possible, the parents should not be kept waiting. They should certainly be offered refreshments.
- Strong emotions can flow at these meetings and you need to be clear and accurate with the facts.
- The meeting is a strategically crucial intervention and every opportunity should be taken to improve the relationship between the school and the family.
- Allow sufficient time for the meeting; be clear about the duration from the start.
- Introduce positive aspects of the child that have progressed over the year and show examples. There are patches of blue sky with virtually every child, so make sure they are mentioned.
- Any changes made to the plan should be clearly listed and agreed by all.

IDEA 33

Meetings after serious incidents

'These meetings are crucial; state exactly what will be discussed and don't stray from the facts.'

Meetings about serious incidents can be difficult, as the responses of some parents can be unpredictable.

Following a serious incident, especially those that result in exclusion, the school will request a meeting with the parents. This should happen as soon as possible after the exclusion or incident occurs, ideally the morning after. During the meeting, you have to be clear about the facts, e.g. when the incident occurred and who was involved. *How* the incident occurred is the next point on the agenda and the child could be asked to describe what happened. The child might be asked to wait outside while the parent is given time to describe:

- what the child said happened
- any incident at home that may have created the behaviour
- any change of personnel at home or change of circumstance
- any other children involved.

It's a good time to listen and not be abrasive; the parent may be experiencing the same behaviour at home. They may be a single parent with little support or could be under significant pressure. Parents certainly don't have the support systems you have in school, nor your experience of managing difficult children, so you should try to be supportive. However, the expectations and requirements of the school must be made clear. A good resolution will maintain the school's ethos and also support parents' understanding of those requirements.

Teaching tip

If handled correctly, a meeting with parents following a serious incident can be a game-changer. Be well prepared.

Bonus idea ★

You should always have available a detailed description of the incident. The description could be presented and the child could be asked to sign the document.

Meeting parents at the gate

'This is a brilliant time to just have a quick chat.'

Parents of children with SEMH don't always see the school as a friendly institution, but just a few words each day may start to break down barriers.

When parents appear in the playground at the beginning or end of the day to deliver or receive their children, there can be a race to talk to you. You are, after all, the parent for the day. Some may have concerns, express thanks for a positive letter home, or just give some details regarding future events. Often the parents of children with SEMH don't get a look-in. There can of course be the occasional altercation regarding a pupil's behaviour, which is generally not very helpful.

The parents of SEMH children are perhaps the ones you most need a quick chat with. Some things to remember:

- This is a difficult time of day – you don't want a long chat; you have to teach, but a quick word might be very helpful.
- The parents of SEMH children do tend to stay on the periphery of the playground and may prefer to drop and leave.
- The SEMH pupil may have run off on the way to school and had to be caught and delivered to you; parents may already be stressed.

There are several ways of using the school gate exchange to your advantage, such as a quick chat if a child's behaviour has been difficult in the day, or as part of a behaviour expectation plan (Idea 54). All this might sound demanding but it needs to be. Good communication between you and the parent can change your classroom from difficult to possible. Bliss comes later!

**Extremely
difficult
behaviours**

Part 6

It's not always your fault

'He never behaves like that with me.' (Mother)

If a pupil comes into your class and starts to be a problem straightaway, read whatever information is available, including their background and family history. Talk to other teachers who have managed the pupil.

Children come into primary school at all levels of maturity and can have social intelligence way below their chronological age. Many find school extremely difficult and some never really come to terms with its demands. They can become morbid, fearful, destructive, aggressive or withdrawn, and may have quite profound attachment difficulties.

Resolving these challenges is not easy and some teachers blame themselves for the behaviour these children display. Teachers, with little support outside the school, now manage greater numbers of children with complex disorders. The skill levels of teachers are tested by these profoundly troubled children.

By reading the child's files, you should gain some knowledge of the background of the child. You should be aware of what they may be going home to each evening. You could meet with the parents. You should be aware of their Early Years experiences. Glean whatever you can from colleagues' knowledge of the family and all that surrounds it.

This is not about searching for an excuse – it's about searching for reasons why some profoundly disturbed SEMH pupils behave the way they do and why, in some cases, they can cause such utter chaos. Their extreme behaviours may be modelled from elsewhere and not created by your management or the environment of your classroom.

Stay objective, be clear about your management and, of course, seek help. The politics of who's to blame can be difficult to manage and are certainly not helpful. When a significant event does occur, ask yourself:

- Was this specific incident unique or similar to other less severe occurrences in your class or elsewhere?
- Has the child's behaviour deteriorated since they came into your class?
- Was the parent defensive or aggressive when talking about an incident?
- Was there a recent problem at home?
- Has there been a change to the child's life outside school?

Bonus idea ★

Don't jump to conclusions too quickly; be objective. Look for the pattern of behaviour during the early or later part of the school day. Which subjects seem to cause the biggest problems? Which other pupils are getting involved?

Learn from your mistakes

'We all make mistakes but we don't always learn from them.'

You are going to be tested by these children. Don't make rash decisions and by doing so increase the problem. STOP, think, analyse, think again and avoid the traps laid out for you.

Teaching tip

You might hear that 'He ran away again but I caught him' or 'Her dad turned up last night' by way of explanation of new or escalating behaviour. Don't be too critical of yourself before you know all the facts.

Profoundly disturbed children often come from inconsistent and erratic homes, where family dynamics are questionable. Physical, emotional and sexual abuse are not uncommon with some more damaged children. Vulnerable children are thermometers of the heat experienced the night before or even just before school.

As there are few external resources available to schools, there are more children with these desperate behaviours in your classroom. Special school places for SEMH pupils are rare, compared with other disabilities. EHCPs often take a long time to complete. Exclusion can make the behaviour worse as the child spends more time in the environment where the behaviour was created!

Bonus idea ★

At the end of each week, think about how you dealt with a difficult pupil. Do you feel that you made progress? Think carefully; perhaps write down the things you got right and the tactics that were successful. 'I WON'T TRY THAT AGAIN' is another list you might keep.

Be objective and analytical about individual behaviour. Note what works and what doesn't in particular situations. Obviously, what doesn't work needs attending to first, as any miscalculations on your part make management even more problematic.

Maintaining your confidence to manage these children is crucial. If, after due consideration, you did make a mistake, then learn from it. But remember, some children are so damaged that, however good you are, they sometimes don't get better. Yes, they have to be managed. Yes, your expectations should remain high, but be realistic about what can be achieved. However difficult these children may be, think positively.

Poor academic self-image

'Oh please sir, we're just havin' a laugh!'

The majority of pupils with SEMH see themselves as failures in school. Their poor academic self-image is maintained by poor academic progress. It hurts and leaves them desperate; they hate it and they strike out at you.

In spite of all we do, most SEMH pupils come to school on edge. Historically, school has not been full of happy experiences. They are tense, apprehensive and expecting problems. Outside school, they can often be 'Jack the Lad', having a smoke on the way to school to show how grown up they are. Because of their life experiences, they can appear to be prematurely independent. They might have to be – to survive! But when they get to school – often with low academic attainment – they are vulnerable. They hate being exposed as incompetent or unable to manage the work set.

Some children start school unable to express themselves clearly due to poor language development. This leads on to poor academic attainment, and as they mature, the gap between themselves and the majority of children becomes more apparent. So perhaps outside school, in the street, the park and around town, they behave provocatively. 'I'm just havin' a laugh', they say. In school, 'havin' a laugh' is not accepted and roaming is not permitted. You then present them with behaviour and learning expectations that they might feel are stupid and unachievable.

The problem of poor academic attainment is more obvious in literacy and numeracy, as these take up a large percentage of the school week. Incident recordings in schools show that 50 per cent of all behaviour incidents took place in English or maths.

Teaching tip

The Elton Report (1989) listed all of the pre-incident behaviours, and little has changed since then – except there are more children with SEMH. Read the report to further your understanding of these children and the behaviours they can exhibit: http://www.educationengland.org.uk/documents/elton/elton1989.html.

Bonus idea ★

Remember that it is often these exposed inadequacies that cause the child to disrupt, deflecting away from the real problem – not being able to do the work. Working to improve their academic self-image will hopefully pay dividends in reducing disruptive behaviour.

Praise

'SEMH pupils hate being seen as inadequate, so just a few positive words can alleviate the tension.'

A lot of pre-emptive behaviour acted out by pupils with SEMH is simply setting the stage for later drama. They are testing you out, waiting for an opportunity to wind you up. They are striking the match to light the firework. So what can you do?

Energy is required from you from the very start of the day. First contact has to be positive. Greet the child using their name. Sometimes just a touch on the shoulder can be a good start. Give them a job to do for you, and praise their effort. If they don't put their coat or bag in the right place don't make *too* big a fuss. Slight deviations can be countered by positive intervention. Here are some phrases to try:

- 'I like the start you made, keep going.' (It might not be brilliant but be positive.)
- 'Like your new shoes, very smart.' (Engage with them personally.)
- 'You worked well yesterday.' (Try to concentrate on what they can do.)
- 'Come and look at this, I think you might like it.' (Break the mood; change their perspective.)

Listen carefully to what the pupil may be worried about. It may be minor but it could be important. An early morning change of activity can be a trigger point because there is movement to manage and the next area of learning might be threatening to the child. Collecting in or giving out work might not be a good idea. You have a mental database of past incidents; avoid repeating your mistakes and keep the heat low. They might be striking the match but you have kept it away from the blue touch paper. The longer you can keep the positives going, the better day you will have.

Love or hate?

'My SEMH pupils see school as a safe place – it's predictable, warm and has a few friendly adults.'

The home environment that children with SEMH come from may be in sharp contrast to the demanding and strict environment of school. Their two worlds can conflict.

Consider these three statements about the same group of children:

- Our SEMH pupils love school: it's warm, fairly consistent, there are some nice adults, a few mates, food, lunchtimes, football, games and sometimes activities they like doing.
- Our SEMH pupils hate school because they can't have a laugh, the work is too difficult and they just hate some of the adults.
- Our SEMH pupils like some aspects of school but have their learnt habitual behaviours forbidden, discouraged and prevented whenever these behaviours arise.

That is the paradox you have to deal with. Children spend roughly 25 hours a week in school, and the rest of the time in the home and its surroundings. It's not my intention to depress you, but to make you aware of the dynamics of the situation you face each day. The hope is that by providing positives in the child's life, the process of education might be less painful for you and your SEMH pupils.

The difficult behaviours learned so early in a child's life *can* be treated; the children *can* settle but they may not always absorb what you would like them to. With good, sound management, many of the more profoundly disturbed children can learn to modify their behaviour in specific environments. That in itself is a major achievement for you both.

Teaching tip

Outside the family, you are the most significant adult the child with SEMH has contact with. If managed carefully, with skill, care and empathy, their behaviour can be contained and the child can learn. The environment of your classroom has to be consistent, fair and with as much of that all-important positivity that you can muster. Of course, I am not suggesting that this is easy to achieve.

High-mobility activities

'Free space and movement have too many options. Our SEMH pupils don't always choose appropriately.'

High-mobility periods such as PE, drama, break and lunchtimes can be almost impossible for SEMH pupils to cope with. These tips will help you manage the children during these times.

During these periods of high mobility, you might find that:

- They can't handle the space or the pace that these lessons generate.
- They can't manage unexpected interactions with other pupils.
- They look for the children who are easy to pick on and bully.
- They look for co-conspirators, who will help them create chaos.
- They run around by themselves, causing problems.

Their behaviour tends to be chaotic because their perception of mobility and the consequent freedom it brings is very different from their peers. High-mobility periods in school present too many options for pupils with SEMH. Their social inadequacy is exposed and they are confused. Choosing the appropriate behaviour would mean compliance, and that's not attractive. Lessons such as PE and drama provide temptations they can't resist.

As a consequence, for some lessons, SEMH pupils need to be given precise and detailed instructions about what they are expected to do. They need a programme (with built-in rewards) that you have discussed with them and they have agreed to. If they get A right, then B will follow and so on. There must always be a carrot *but* it must be earned.

There should also be consequences if they don't comply.

- Give clear expectations regarding behaviour at the beginning of the lesson.
- If they abuse the freedom that high mobility allows, time out of the activity for a short period may be a good idea.
- Let them watch and ask to join in when they feel ready.
- Don't exclude them from participation; keep the carrot in view but make it clear what is expected.

Bonus idea ★

Where compliance is proving difficult, find a place or part of the activity that is still important but which requires less movement. This might be easier for them.

Are you predictable?

'Using a variety of responses to similar behaviours keeps pupils guessing.'

Consistently deal with difficulties, but don't be predictable with your response.

Teaching tip

Remember, in school pupils with SEMH feel vulnerable – deep down they want to be like the other children but don't like to show it with immediate compliance. They know they are behaving badly but don't know how to stop. This is paradoxical but so are they. Give them a way out. They like to be part of things but make all the wrong choices, so catch them when they are working well with other children and say something like, 'Wow, I like how well this group is working together.'

There is a likelihood that our pupils are going to place you in a disciplinary mode before too long. How you deal with that is crucial to prevent multiple recurrences of the same behaviour, which tend to increase in severity. The child's behaviour is predictable – they know they are behaving badly and you will have to deal with it! – but yours shouldn't be. You must have an array of responses that put them on the wrong foot. This requires a team effort by staff in the classroom and, where necessary, senior support staff.

You have to be subtle and creative if you're going to succeed. Your response might come under the general description of 'vector therapy', meaning that you don't direct the response at the problem but go at an angle to the difficulty. As soon as a problem is detected, redirect the activity; make a break with what's expected and act. Go in at an angle to the behaviour and deflect the build-up. Here are some examples of how you might approach a problem from an unexpected angle:

- 'Well done, yep, I know the problem, so let's look at this, just come over here.'
- 'Wow, just had an idea. Go with Miss Brown and look at the wall display down the corridor. When you come back, tell me what you think.'
- 'Let's go and have a look at what X [another pupil] has done.'

- 'Yep, seen that, let's go to my desk and see what the internet says.'
- 'That work you did the other day was really good. Remember the drawing of the boat? Just brilliant.'

SEMH pupils are waiting for you to do the usual thing when they behave in a particular way. They *know* that their behaviour is going to wind you up, then you respond in a predictable way and off we go to the next miserable step. This can be extremely gratifying for them, as they are managing *your* behaviour (response). If you continually make the same response, your classroom management can become 'a bit of a laugh'. You really can't allow that to happen.

Bonus idea ★

Think creatively; try some role play with colleagues or friends. Set up a situation and ask someone to model a specific behaviour. Respond to the behaviour as if you were in the classroom. Ask your colleague or friend how that felt. Try the same behaviour again with a different response and repeat. It can be great fun and perhaps you might end up having a bit of a laugh, but it's all about smartening up your act and making sure you are not predictable.

If punishment worked...

'How dare you speak to me like that – go straight to the time-out room!'

Pupils with SEMH often see punishment as an acknowledgement and reward for their provocative behaviour. If punishment is repeated, it hardens their sense of rejection and increases the likelihood of them repeating the behaviours. If it's that obvious, why do teachers occasionally reach for that negative solution and what can they do differently?

Teaching tip

If you approach difficult behaviours as an intellectual challenge rather than just a frustrating part of your day, you will improve your skill dramatically. If you plod on with the same negative responses, you will get angry and the pupil with SEMH will enjoy watching it happen.

Unfortunately, some teachers can jump straight to 'punishment' because these difficult children can occasionally drive teachers to respond in a negative way. It doesn't work, but at the time teachers need to release the tension these children generate. The problem arises when punishment is seen as a way of changing behaviour. If punishment did provide a solution, then the number of SEMH pupils would be reduced virtually overnight!

A frustrated teacher might use punitive tactics, e.g. 'Don't you dare do that. You will now miss your breaktimes', when frustrated by particular behaviours. When teachers respond in this way, the children are getting just what they expected – rejection!

Uncompromising, dismissive and negative remarks *reward* negative behaviour. Correction has to have a therapeutic element and has to be meaningful to the pupil.

- Shouting out? Find a quiet place and insist on quiet talking with a TA.
- Out of seat? Sit quietly with a teacher at breaktime and have a chat.
- Threatening a pupil? Bring pupils together, include all the participants and discuss.

- Damaging property? Children must be part of the replacement process, e.g. taking a chair to the office, taping up a damaged book.

If a response is not linked to the behaviour, it is a 'punishment'. Restorative responses such as these are initially hard work but there is that essential link between the behaviour and the consequence. If you start to consistently make the link between behaviour and consequence, the behaviour is more likely to be resolved. Both you and the pupil benefit from the curative nature of the intervention.

Bonus idea ★

Make a list of all the repeating behaviours you have to manage regularly. Now write down what you usually do about those behaviours. Choose one to work on, e.g. pupils talking when you are addressing the whole class. Write down what you usually do. Now list three different strategies you could use and try them out. If you are inventive, it can be fun. Link your responses to the behaviour and see whether the behaviour lessens.

Triggers

'It's a bit like watching a float when fishing; any little dip or movement sideways warns you about what's going on under the surface!'

There are a multitude of triggers that spark difficult behaviour; some of them are specific to an individual child. Therefore, it is important to learn quickly what sparks the unwanted behaviour.

Taking it further

Viewing SEMH pupils objectively is essential; if you become subjective, you may start mimicking the child's behaviour. Remember that they have a profound disability, which can only be lessened by good practice and clear objectives. If you catch virtually any disturbance early enough, the prognosis is more positive. If you can find the root of the problem in relation to the functioning of your class, you can put measures in place that alleviate the difficulties.

Spotting the triggers:

- At the beginning of a lesson, scan the room and check how settled the pupils with SEMH appear (Idea 17).
- Are they already reacting irritably to people around them?
- Are they upset by something beyond their immediate environment?
- Are they quieter than usual? (Never a good sign!)

Activities that may cause problems:

- chaotic changes of activity
- English and maths
- backtracking on a subject
- moving around the classroom or school
- breaktime
- any delay in the flow of teaching
- visitors to the classroom
- the teacher having to leave the classroom.

Try to stay close and involve the pupil in conversation to glean what you can about how they are feeling. Immediately deal with any sign of irritation, resolve negative remarks and be aware of other children who might be attempting to wind up the SEMH pupil. Most of all, be vigilant.

There are occasions when there appears to be no obvious trigger for an unwanted behaviour. These can be caused by a build-up of internal anxieties; there may be flashbacks that the child is unable to resolve, causing internal conflict; or it may be a behaviour that has become habitual, with many causes. Such incidents are not easy to anticipate but the quicker you get to know your SEMH children, the more likely you are to anticipate incidents and resolve them quickly before escalation.

If angry children are not protected from triggers, or have unresolved triggers, then they are likely to escalate their negative behaviours.

Triggers are covered in more detail in Part 9.

It could be your fault

'Some teachers just don't seem to get it right; for that tiny minority, life can be hell.'

Teaching, as a profession, has become extremely demanding — not just because of the required administration, record-keeping and daily preparation, but because of the increasing number of SEMH pupils. Teaching is not a profession that can be entered into lightly.

This is not easy to say, but it is true — sometimes, teachers can create problems through inappropriate management. Teachers can cause a child to escalate their behaviour when they miscalculate, get tired or become exasperated by a child or group of children.

- Teachers may start a lesson or even a day already tense. They may have personal problems.
- They may be anxious about the management of a particular child or even the class. These genuine anxieties can cause the teacher to respond too quickly to an incident in a disproportionate way, causing the pupil — who may also be tense — to erupt.
- Some teachers simply don't have the skills required to defuse an escalating situation. They say the wrong thing at the wrong time. Consequently, the child spins out of control.
- Confronting a child and leaving them no options can cause a situation to heat up. Teachers offering only one option, such as 'do as you are told' (often repeated, with an increasing volume), leave nowhere for the child to go, and this situation can, in some cases, become violent.
- Teachers who are inconsistent can be seen as unfair by SEMH children. What is a rule one day is relaxed the next. What appears to be

okay for one child is not okay for our SEMH pupils.

- Ironically, some teachers can almost hide in the classroom. They press on with a lesson, ignoring the build-up.
- Unfortunately, incompetent teachers can blame the child.

The scenarios presented above are intentionally stark. But beware: there may be aspects of these behaviours present in your own teaching. Seek out the advice and support of your colleagues and be reflective about your own practice.

Taking it further

If you are consistently getting it wrong with a pupil, group or class, go back to basics and think objectively about your practice. Don't just plough on. Reorganise, change your style, rethink your attitude and revisit your interventions. Talk about the difficulties; don't hide them away.

Take-up time

'Wait before you intervene to give the children a chance to settle.'

When SEMH pupils are feeling sensitive (which is most of the time) and they commit a small misdemeanour at the beginning of the lesson, don't draw immediate attention to it with a public reprimand. This is especially important if it is the first time you have communicated with them in the lesson.

Teaching tip

These children demand high energy and constant positive attention. The more positives you put in, the more effective the corrective intervention can be. Just a warning: don't over-praise when the effort by the child is poor; they know you are playing a game.

Avoid reinforcing a negative behaviour by drawing attention to it and increasing the probability of it reoccurring. However, make sure the pupil is aware that you know what has happened. There are times when minor incidents are better ignored or just marked by a glance. After all, the pupil is probably just testing your nerve and patience and, of course, as a good teacher, you have infinite nerve and patience!

There is a thin and subtle line between jumping in too quickly and not reacting quickly enough; it's all in the timing. Teachers sometimes follow an opening reprimand with another in quick succession if compliance is not immediate. This can be irritating for the pupil and bad behaviour can then escalate rapidly.

The solution is to give a little take-up time: once you have asked for compliance, just pause and wait for the pupil to respond. This is simply about allowing a few seconds to elapse following your glance or gesture to give the pupil time to settle. It ensures that they do not feel threatened by your first request for better behaviour.

Keeping things calm

Part 7

Entering the classroom

'Start as you mean to go on.'

Beginning a lesson punctually is crucial. It sends the message to all your pupils that you — the teacher — are ready to start and there is work to be done.

Don't begin a lesson by having to recover control. Use these tips to help you start a lesson well:

- There must be quiet (not necessarily silence) before the class is allowed to enter. Make sure everyone is calm and under control.
- No running, pushing, loud talking or bad language should be permitted during this crucial phase. If it happens, stop what is happening and start again. The pupils will tire of this boring repetition well before you do.
- Pathways to desks and tables should be unimpeded and understood by everyone. Make sure your seating plans are obeyed.
- Make strong contact with your pupils by reminding them about your expectations at the beginning of lessons.
- Everyone is expected to be on time, with no latecomers. Remind persistent stragglers of the consequences of lateness. No individual or group of pupils should keep you and the rest of the class waiting. Remind them that being late is bad-mannered, unacceptable and very inconvenient for everyone.

Achieving silence

'There is only one kind of silence – TOTAL!'

It is essential to start every new phase of the day with silent 'eyes on me'. It's a clear marker that signals 'I am in charge'. It's not megalomania; it's teaching.

Learning a quick, calm and quiet way of achieving silence is one of the best tools in your teaching skills bag. I have observed some classes where the teacher asks for silence, and I am still waiting for it to happen! Here are some ways to *achieve* silence:

- Stand arms folded, scanning the room (my favourite).
- Quietly, repeatedly ask for silence (if you're repeating too many times, it's not working).
- Raise your hand and signal to all silent members of the class to do the same.
- Ask everyone initially to stand and then seat them when they are silent (this is a good settler if you can achieve it).
- Insist on silence from the beginning (in certain circumstances).
- A special rhythmic clap, which all the children copy (most used).

Order at the beginning means more chance of order in the middle and at the end. Entering and leaving the classroom should always be calm and uneventful. Remember that our SEMH pupils may have been free to roam at breaktime so they may be a bit flushed. Don't forget the end of a lesson. How you finish a phase of teaching is hugely important because an orderly conclusion can affect how you start the next phase, especially at breaks and lunchtimes. Conclude your teaching, achieve silence and then release in a controlled way. This leaves an imprint of your authority, which can last until the children return.

Teaching tip

Achieving silence is only a small part of the management of these troubled children but can help them to feel like a member of a controlled group.

Bonus idea ★

The routine has to be conducted and managed by you. So, you have to be there before the children arrive – no extra natter at lunch or breaktime.

Positive intervention

'Being positive and directing with a smile is very therapeutic.'

When the behaviour of our pupils with SEMH is getting a bit frayed, you might start with a gentle, positive intervention.

Here are some example phrases you might use when children are just starting to become unsettled:

- 'You have worked well so far, don't spoil it.'
- 'I'll come and see you in a minute, looks good from here.'
- 'Nice try, yep, probably should have given you this to do.'
- 'That's not so bad, just change that; don't throw away all that good work, come on.'

This is a low-key, non-threatening intervention if spoken in a calm, quiet voice. Give take-up time; don't expect immediate obedience – just let it sink in and keep an eye on the situation. The tone of your voice is crucial. Do not be gentle but certainly don't be abrasive. Choose your words carefully and be clear about what is expected.

- Give only brief eye contact – just a glance but directed straight at the child's eyes.
- Don't smile. That's like asking the child whether it's okay for you to intervene!
- Walk away – perhaps turn your back, signalling that you expect your request to be followed.
- Don't rush into more eye contact after the intervention.

If the behaviour starts to bubble up again, move a little closer to the child. Look over their shoulder and make a non-committal noise, e.g. 'mm' or cough, and just stay there briefly. When you move on, not a word has been spoken, but the child knows exactly what you mean.

Preventative intervention

'Be clear: certainly not aggressive, but make it obvious what is required.'

A preventative intervention is a step up from a positive intervention. It's the next tool in your toolbox.

An escalation can start if you become too abrupt too soon, so start gently with one of these phrases:

- 'I got the groups wrong; perhaps next time I need to separate you two?'
- 'Hey, that's a bit noisy. Just be a bit quieter, I'll work with you.'
- 'I think it might be better if you worked over here.'
- 'I know you can work better than that, take more care.'
- 'I would like you to finish this piece of work, so settle down.'

Be careful: you are not making a demand, you are stating a fact. Our SEMH pupils know exactly what they are doing; they are challenging you by ignoring your positive intervention. Use one of the preventative intervention phrases above, then pause, look puzzled, and give yourself time to think. The difficult pupil might be thinking, 'What's the teacher going to do?' They know the teacher has to do something. Other children in the class may be watching you to see what you do. If the child hasn't responded to your preventative intervention:

- State the fact: 'It's a problem for the class'.
- Don't raise your voice; keep your body still and arms loose.
- No eyeballing the child in question – just the occasional glance.
- Don't get *too* close but get close enough.
- If the behaviour doesn't change, then repeat the fact.
- Stay calm, with nice relaxed shoulders.

Teaching tip

Use 'I need', 'I will', 'I think', 'I know' or 'I would' to mark the behaviour and be directional.

Taking it further

Resolving this situation is now dependent on how difficult the child intends to be, which can sometimes hang on what has previously occurred in the classroom. If preventative intervention is not working, move on to Idea 51.

Drawing a red line intervention

'Stay calm, clear and strong, stating the behaviour expected without any negotiation.'

If positive and preventative interventions haven't reduced the problem, then the behaviour is obviously more acute. The child is presenting you with a clear challenge. The disruption is preventing you from teaching and the child wants your attention.

Teaching tip

Remember with all interventions that you must always give time for your stated expectation to take effect (see Idea 46).

Get reasonably close but not too close and say, 'Okay that's enough, you need to calm down.' You may get a negative response. Repeat the request but don't raise your voice; you could go down a register. Don't wait for a response; just walk away and give it time to sink in.

- Perhaps work with the pupil next to the SEMH child so you can be near to them. 'Shhhhhh, listen carefully, I am trying to teach and I am finding it very difficult. I can help you with your work, so just settle down now; I'll be with you in a second or two'.
- Ask the whole class to be quiet. Achieve silence, start again and move over to the child you're targeting. Say clearly to the whole class, 'Okay, we are all quiet. Now just get on with your work.'
- Then give the child a bit of time and support as the others work quietly.

Bonus idea ★

It is important that there is no shouting. If you shout, you are fanning the flames and losing credibility. Think before you speak, get the words and tone right, add a little bit more eye contact and be clear about your demands.

With more demanding interventions such as this one, you should be more direct with your language: 'calm down', 'just settle down now', 'get on with your work'. You are clear, directive and require a change of behaviour. If the behaviour continues, this has to be the final instruction before you act. The language is different from the previous interventions: no compromise, no positives, clear demands and short and sweet.

Marginal children who like creating trouble

'Spot the children on the margins; they enjoy turning the heat up.'

You can be more direct with some children. They know what they are doing and by identifying their strategies early on, you can prevent a major class disturbance.

Sometimes, the escalation of behaviour can be brought about by the interaction between two or more pupils who may not have SEMH difficulties. Pupils with SEMH are easily led and easily wound up. There are some pupils who are not in themselves too hard to manage, but who will always enjoy a disturbance, and can go out of their way to develop one. They are the fringe players: 'marginal' children, who can hover around, engineering potential disasters, unless spotted and checked by you.

These marginal children are not as sensitive or vulnerable as the more challenging children, so you can be much more direct with them. Make it clear that you are aware of their intentions and that you won't tolerate their behaviour. Make it clear what the consequences will be.

They will no doubt proclaim their innocence – 'What, me?' – and perhaps even complain that you're picking on them. Ignore this subterfuge; it is just designed to distract you. They know exactly what they are doing.

Ensure marginal pupils sit well away from your SEMH pupils and out of eye contact. If children in this category come into class as a group, split the group up straightaway and don't allow networks to reform (see Idea 19). If, after being warned, they make remarks that are likely to provoke, be quick to correct, with a clear, direct request offering no second chance.

Teaching tip

Always be fair and keen to prevent injustices because all the pupils in your class will admire and respect you for that. Most children know exactly what you are doing and why, and will appreciate your interventions.

Structures that stop things happening

Part 8

Know your ABCs

'ABC is a really good, objective way of improving your behaviour management skills.'

The antecedents, behaviour, consequence (ABC) model is a straightforward way of analysing behaviour. It makes the dynamics of behaviour easier to understand and places behaviour in the context of past, present and future.

The **antecedents** are the precursors to the behaviour, which may have contributed to creating the behaviour. These could include triggers and other aspects of the immediate environment or elsewhere. The **behaviours** are caused by the antecedents. The **consequences** are what follow the behaviour.

Think back over recent incidents and see whether there were common antecedents. Following the behaviour incidents, were there any consequences for the pupil? If so, did the consequence prevent a reoccurrence of the behaviour? These are basic questions to ask using this simple model.

The ABC model is not a silver bullet but might assist your thinking when attempting to resolve a repetitive behaviour. Antecedents-behaviour-consequence can in some cases become cyclical. If nothing changes, i.e. the antecedents are not modified, the behaviour occurs and/or the consequences remain ineffective, then the behaviour will be repeated.

Keep a simple record of incidents for a defined period of time. Can you link the behaviour with the antecedents? You may notice some patterns in your data. You can use this same record to track whether your interventions are having an impact. Here is an example:

Name Brian				Date 21/06/18	
	Antecedents	Behaviour	Consequence	Is there a link?	What needs to change?
1	Start of an English lesson	Getting angry, swearing at another pupil	Asked to wait outside the classroom for five minutes	He can get upset when an English lesson starts, he is a poor reader	Change the way English lesson is delivered, better differentiation
2	At the start of the next English lesson, present less threatening task	Quieter but still a bit agitated	Ask a TA to support Brian	He is quieter	Perhaps start Brian off with a TA for support at the start of the lesson?

Bonus idea ★

At the end of a teaching phase or at the end of the day, you can ask the pupil what they think. It could develop into a healthy discussion and perhaps help them to understand why they get so anxious.

Creating a behaviour expectation plan

'Identify the behaviours you want to reduce; don't start with the toughest.'

When one of your SEMH children has ongoing high-frequency behaviours that constantly stop you from teaching, something has to be done. A behaviour expectation plan (BEP) can be one of the ways to reduce those continuing behaviours.

Great care has to be taken when setting up a behaviour expectation plan.

- You have to be clear about what behaviours are preventing you from teaching.
- Your descriptions of the behaviours have to be specific.
- Share the description with the pupil involved and, where possible, with the parents.
- Perhaps use a serious incident as a reason to create the plan.
- Make other staff aware of the plan, including TAs and auxiliary staff who may have to deal with the pupil.

If there are a variety of behaviours that you constantly have to deal with, try the following suggestions:

- Make a list of six behaviours and place them in a hierarchy from extremely difficult to difficult.
- Discuss the list with the pupil; listen carefully to their thoughts and opinions.
- Between you, agree on one behaviour to change and set a time limit to achieve this.
- Discuss a reward.

You might think, 'Why can't we tackle more than one behaviour?' Well, we are going to eat this elephant a spoonful at a time. It's a bit of a trick really because what usually happens is that if you resolve one behaviour, another one of the six also disappears! The alternative is trying to change *all* the behaviours and that's doomed to failure with many of our SEMH pupils.

When the behaviour and the reward have been agreed, the pupil, parents and you should sign a posh-looking document. Set the start date, usually for the following day, and then off you go.

Remember that a BEP has to have a time limit, e.g. reviewed at the end of the week. If the behaviour selected reduces significantly, send a positive letter off to the parents with lots of fanfare. Now think about other behaviours. Discuss with the pupil and see what they think. What you might be getting into is a discussion about behaviour rather than a shouting match – this dialogue is the curative factor, along with the rewards.

Bonus idea ★

When choosing the behaviour to work on changing, don't select the most difficult behaviour. Pick one from the middle of your hierarchy, or pick a behaviour that is more convenient for you to manage and easier to reward.

Immediately after an incident

'Disturbed behaviour is like seeing one tip of an iceberg – underneath lie many more behaviours waiting to surface.'

Once a SEMH pupil's behaviour has started to bubble, it is very difficult for them to calm down completely. They are wound up, and in most cases a residue of agitation can remain, so it's important to remain calm and be careful at this point.

If another incident occurs shortly after your intervention about another matter, it can be doubly difficult to manage. The child can begrudge your intervention and look for another opportunity to disrupt. Therefore, you have to think creatively about how you and your SEMH pupils can relate without friction.

- Straight after an incident is a vulnerable time for pupils with SEMH – take care.
- If the behaviour has subsided and instructions are followed, just give it time. Don't rush into praising too quickly, don't try to become a mate, just let the child slowly calm down.
- Keep to normal expectations.
- Non-verbal communication might be considered: a smile, a nod of the head or even a thumbs up might be appropriate. Don't overdo it!
- Keep low-key verbal communication to a minimum.
- Occasional eye contact, perhaps just a glance, may be appropriate.

When all is quiet, you can return to normal conversation. Look for something to praise, but don't overdo it. As time passes and if the behaviour has not reoccurred, you can make a few changes.

- Regroup a few children but don't only move the difficult child, because they might feel singled out.
- Standing next to the SEMH pupil, stop and reiterate the learning target to the whole class.
- Address the whole class and say how well everybody is now working.

The target now is to get to the end of the learning phase relatively unscathed. Getting out of this time interval intact makes the next one easier. So, to finish the lesson in good order:

- Try to keep noise and movement down to a minimum.
- Collect up materials and equipment but don't ask the SEMH child to do that!
- Dismiss the class in a controlled, orderly way; try not to leave your SEMH pupil until last.
- If possible, as the pupil leaves the room, make a positive remark.

'Finish well, start afresh' should be your motto. It's great if you can achieve it because life can get that bit easier; it increases your confidence in your own ability to manage and improves your teaching skill. Learning from your mistakes is equally important.

Bonus idea ★

Preventing an escalation can increase your blood pressure and you may look a bit frazzled. Drop your shoulders, stand tall, speak normally and calm down – the children are watching you. If you look troubled, the child with SEMH might think it's time to wind you up.

Creating class rules

'Every child has a right to be educated in a calm, settled environment.'

Give time to this activity. It should be all-inclusive and owned by all the children, class adults and parents. Get it right and everybody has a clear, sound manifesto.

Teaching tip

If the process of creating class rules is managed skilfully and used as group therapy for all pupils and adults, it becomes a powerful document. You can use it and see it as a backbone to hang good behaviour on.

You must generate the right atmosphere and devote time in which to develop rules with the class. The rules should be based around the need for you to teach in an interesting and uninterrupted way.

Plan a lesson or part of a lesson around 'rule building'. State clearly why the rules are important and why you want the pupils to participate in the process. Stress the importance of good behaviour and why all pupils should be clear about shared class values. This is an excellent opportunity to include SEMH pupils in the discussion. Ask them to express their views openly about what they see as good and bad behaviour.

Typically, most pupils like a classroom to be well ordered, relaxed and interesting. They don't like chaos and they hate challenging behaviour. So, use this to shape the framework for the rules. Carefully organise everybody's thinking by channelling their ideas into economic statements of expectation – rules, in other words.

Bonus idea ★

Rules should be positive – the 'dos', not the 'don'ts'. 'Don'ts' can be a brilliant set of targets for disruptive children to transgress! For example, 'Don't talk when the teacher is talking' might be better expressed as 'When anyone is talking to the class, we should all listen.'

Only develop a small number of rules, e.g. five to eight. A long list can be confusing and boring, as can making individual rules too long. Avoid using vague generalities like, 'We must all try to be friends'. 'We expect good manners at all times' might be more achievable.

Using class rules

'If you get class rules right, it is an extra tool in your skills bag.'

You have to like and understand the process of making and using class rules. If you feel it's another thing you have to do, then perhaps it's not for you — you have to be invested.

Give every pupil a copy of the rules and send a copy to all parents with a return slip attached. Instruct parents to confirm that they have read them and invite them to comment on the rules. If slips are not returned, send a second copy, this time by post. If you are going to have rules, they should be known and accepted by everyone.

Make sure that everyone clearly understands the rules once they have been agreed and written down. Type up the rules and frame them in a prominent place. You could get the whole class to sign them. Get all the children to write them out and decorate their posters, then make a display of them.

You now have a short set of rules that have been unanimously agreed and owned by everyone. If a child with SEMH difficulties steps out of line, their behaviour is targeted not against just you, but against the will of classmates and parents.

You need to review the rules on a regular basis and not leave them to go stale. If your display is damaged in any way, replace it with a new pristine copy immediately.

Teaching tip

If you are not keen on this idea, don't use it. If you think it might work, then put some effort into it, because if you are not enthusiastic, it won't work for the class.

Bonus idea ★

With some behaviours, you might be able to point to the rules on the wall without saying a single word and the behaviour may subside.

IDEA 58

Individual rewards

'A positive remark, a tiny smiling face or a special positive mark in a book is nurturing.'

Behaviour can only be changed by rewarding positively wherever possible. That doesn't just apply to SEMH children but applies to the whole class.

I once conducted a survey of Year 6 children regarding their knowledge of the rewards and punishment systems running in the school. I interviewed ten children who had been identified by staff as SEMH and ten identified as non-SEMH. I was horrified to discover that the SEMH pupils were very aware of the punishment system but had no knowledge of the reward system. The non-SEMH pupils were very knowledgeable about the reward system but had no knowledge of the punishment system. These were two entirely separate communities in the same school – even the same class!

Think about your class. Ask yourself whether such a division might exist in your own classroom. Are there one or two children who are rarely rewarded but often reprimanded? Do the majority know only rewards? What do you think the children with SEMH think about that?

You might think that's how things are. It's like saying the rich get richer and the poor, oh well, they just get poorer.

If any child, regardless of disability, only experiences negative signals, they will feel undervalued and possibly become quite distressed. The more isolated and disturbed children just give up on the idea of rewards and, in certain circumstances, quite enjoy the negative because at least they get noticed!

Individual recognition of good behaviour can be a device you can use to improve behaviour. Take a photo of every child and when they make a contribution to the class, put their photo on the wall. Pupils with SEMH will want to get a posting in the same way that most children will.

Following an individual's good behaviour, a positive message could be sent home in the form of a text message, an email or a handwritten note. This can be used as a special device for children with SEMH difficulties. A bright postcard works really well too.

Bonus idea

You may need to cheat a bit and give SEMH pupils the odd reward when they just about deserve it. The majority of children will know what you are doing. Don't cheat too much, though, or you will be spotted and the whole thing could fall flat.

Class rewards

'Peer pressure formalised can be therapeutic.'

A little bit of peer pressure in the form of a class reward system can help children with SEMH to check some of their less serious behaviour.

Class reward systems can take many forms and the rewards themselves may be varied. The system has to be clear and understood by all the pupils, not just a majority. Start by listing a variety of whole-class behaviours to be rewarded. Be clear about what is expected. Here are some suggestions:

- a good, well-behaved teaching phase
- all-round good concentration
- well-behaved movement around the school
- good assembly presentation
- everyone sitting quietly in assembly
- keeping the classroom tidy
- another member of staff remarking on the class's good behaviour.

Have a class discussion and see whether the pupils want to add something else. Put a class behaviour chart on the wall with smiling faces or stars. For a set number of symbols, the class gets a reward – or, better still, surprise the class with a treat! A great positive of this idea is that SEMH pupils may feel a bit of pressure from the whole class.

Triggers

Part 9

Out of the blue

'You can't always predict why these children blow without warning.'

Understanding the triggers a child may be facing can help you to understand the whole child.

Pupils with SEMH difficulties are sensitive; you may find it hard to believe but it's true. That's why the triggers they respond to make them jump higher than most children. Some examples of triggers that can cause an escalation are:

- Bad news at home, from friends or an event in sub-culture, football or the family.
- Criticism, e.g. negative remarks about clothes, hair, shoes or handwriting.
- Feeling that something bad is going to happen, e.g. bullying, going home to trouble, wetting the bed and not telling anybody, mum going into hospital.
- Something threatening, e.g. school work, homework, spelling tests, SATs, dad coming home.
- Intimidation from teacher, TA, another child or at home from parents, carers or siblings.
- Disappointment, e.g. poor test results, football cancelled, unfulfilled promises.
- Self-esteem damaged, e.g. public humiliation, rejection by a friend, spots, soiling themselves.
- Expectations not fulfilled, e.g. poor performance, favourite lesson cancelled, rejection by a mate, not going on school trip.
- Irritation, e.g. other children winding them up, calling them names or making noises.

Some of these are small things while others are major events, but to SEMH pupils, they are all difficult to manage. It's not always possible to anticipate explosions, but be ready to respond when they occur.

Calm words

'Appear calm – be low key but clear. No ambiguity, no wavering, no demands.'

When SEMH pupils are responding to triggers, it is important that you get the style and tone of your speech correct.

On these difficult occasions, your heartbeat increases, your blood pressure increases and your breathing might quicken, and this can affect your speech. Try to speak slowly; control your breathing and pronounce your words carefully.

By speaking slowly, you are expressing the seriousness of the situation. It also gives you time to think and plan what comes next. Any inappropriate remark or too heavy emphasis on obedience can cause a major disruption.

When a child with SEMH is beginning to lose control, they listen to your tone and the vocabulary you are using. They assess the level of stress they cause you; any sign of anxiety or stress on your part can only heighten the chances of a further, more dangerous challenge.

Keep calm. Plan what you are going to say and measure the responses you get. Then gauge the effectiveness of your interventions. You're like a triage nurse in A&E. Think: does this child need to be rushed away or can we just wait and see how they are? You are checking on them to work out what treatment is required. You need to assess what would be the best way of resolving their problem while keeping yourself calm.

Teaching tip

You need to be sharp-witted and think tactically, not emotionally. Don't flap your arms about; use a quiet body and calm voice. I know that's not always easy!

IDEA 62

Trigger kicks off

'Avoid falling into an immediate and too negative response.'

When behaviour becomes more than a low-level irritation and threatens to escalate, treat the symptom, not the cause.

For SEMH pupils, triggers can be the start of an escalation, which ends with you taking the full heat of the temper. Most children try to avoid triggers by looking away, ignoring and getting on with their work. Some pupils with SEMH look for triggers to wind themselves up; you might hear them say, 'Stop him from looking at me, he's winding me up.'

When pupils reach a state of high tension, you have to listen very carefully to what they are saying because somewhere in the middle of the shouting and mumbling is a clue. Pay attention to everything that is being said; don't pass judgment but occasionally ask for a bit of calm and clarity. There may be swearing – don't demand that it should stop, just ask if it could be lessened.

If you make any outright demands, *you* will become the problem instead of the initial source of the anxiety. Avoid asking what the problem is and just concentrate on the behaviour itself.

Give an assurance that whatever it is, it can be solved but only in a calm and well-mannered way. Throughout this process, it is advisable to move closer to the pupil without touching them. Stay at a distance that feels comfortable for both of you. Keep reminding them that no one has been hurt and the problem can be solved. Normally, distressed pupils' anxieties will come in waves, so don't expect a smooth journey. Wait for the small waves and use them to assure the troubled child that all is safe.

Teaching tip

It's important to retain contact with the rest of the class and maintain the momentum of the lesson, like keeping plates spinning on a stick. As things calm down, increase your contact with the class but maintain clear contact with the troubled pupil, as little bubbles of anger can appear from time to time. Just move away a bit, but be very watchful.

Bonus idea ★

Be especially wary of any marginal pupils in the class who like dramas and will provoke the pupil with SEMH. You could ask those pupils to wait outside until calm is restored. When the SEMH pupil is eventually calm, make sure the marginal pupils know how you feel about their unhelpful intervention.

Keeping the class in check

'At all times scan the rest of the class and keep them on task.'

Ensure that you monitor the rest of the class whenever a child with SEMH is having difficulties. Remind the whole class of the purpose and aims of your lesson.

When a child with SEMH is becoming difficult, you will need to balance their needs and behaviour with the needs and behaviour of the rest of the class. First, check the pupils who are sitting close to the troubled child:

- Are they involved? Could they be the cause?
- Are they being brought into the situation?
- Are they in any sort of danger?
- Are they disturbed by the situation?

Check the mood of the class and keep them on task:

- Make a quick scan of the whole class.
- Reiterate the task that has been set.
- Ask them to put their hands up if they have a problem.
- Prompt any other child who has become unsettled to return to their work.

This is not just about reassuring the class that you are calm and in control; you are also signalling to the troubled child that normal service is still going on. Don't wave your arms around; keep quite still and gradually the emotions will subside.

As soon as there is a lull in the behaviour, use it to move the class on and include the troubled pupil in the comments and direction. Slowly return to being the director of the class and not just the manager of our troubled child. Again, you have to be careful – don't rush to this stage too quickly but aim for a resolution.

Teaching tip

The pupil with SEMH may be feeling isolated. They are losing control and paradoxically want you to resolve it. In most cases you can orchestrate a successful outcome, but you must stay calm.

Bonus idea ★

Don't make any damning or derogatory remarks about the troubled child; that will turn the class against the pupil, or possibly against you.

What not to say

'Don't get into a string of negative bickering; it makes things much worse.'

The language and tone you use sends a clear message. The right tone can de-escalate a situation; the wrong tone can make it worse.

Don't be rigid and overbearing. Go *around* the behaviour and find a way to correct it without demanding immediate submission. Whatever you do, avoid pomposity – your professional competence isn't being challenged.

Look at the two scripts below. One is clearly more successful than the other, but why?

Exchange 1
Teacher: 'Don't do that, Brian.'
Pupil: 'What? I'm not doing anything!'
Teacher: 'That silly noise.'
Pupil: 'What noise? I wasn't making a noise.'
Teacher: 'Brian, I saw you making it.'
Pupil: 'Oh you saw me making a noise, that's clever.' [some of the class laugh]
Teacher: 'You're upsetting David.'
Pupil: 'I wasn't.'
Teacher: 'Yes you were.'
Pupil: 'I was not. What are you going to do about it then?'

Exchange 2
Teacher: 'Brian.'
Pupil: 'Yes, Miss?'
Teacher: 'You know.'
Pupil: 'What?'
Teacher: 'That noise.'
Pupil: 'What noise, Miss?'
Teacher: 'Do it again, Brian.'
Pupil: 'Faaaaaart.' [class laughs]
Teacher: 'Thanks Brian, let's get on.'

Bonus idea ★

Try to think, 'She's having a laugh' and not 'How dare she behave like that in my class?' Yes, the pupil shouldn't be 'having a laugh' but be creative with your thinking. Try disciplining with humour rather than anger; anger can make you look weak.

By drawing red lines too soon, you might be adding fuel to the fire. Consider the way the responses are delivered. The second script is not threatening; it's not generating heat and Brian might even laugh about it.

Be clear about the cause

'SEMH covers a whole spectrum of disorders.'

When SEMH pupils get anxious, they start to behave badly. Whatever caused the behaviour might be not just the trigger but an unresolved anxiety. The social, emotional and mental health challenges that SEMH pupils face generate the unwanted behaviour, rather than the other way around.

To better understand children with SEMH, let's look at other challenged children who may also be in your class:

Children with significant physical disorders may have a problem getting into school, moving around the classroom, holding a pen, keeping their head still or speaking.

Autistic children may have problems with relationships or following normal school procedures. They may say inappropriate things or become extremely agitated when things don't go as they think they should. They can become social isolates.

Children with dyslexia may find spelling very difficult, reading painfully slow and comprehension often impossible.

When SEMH pupils create problems, it's because they have a problem defined as a social, emotional or mental health difficulty. It's the triggers we have to deal with, but it's the disorder that causes the problem. It's their way of responding to you, the school, the man on the street, their parents and everybody they meet. The most profoundly damaged children can't behave in any other way! The triggers expose the problem, just like stairs create a problem for children with physical disorders. All the triggers, staff, parents and the environment stimulate the behaviour, which then has to be dealt with.

Teaching tip

You should always aim to understand *why* a problem is recurring. The behaviour is an expression of the child's inability to cope with a particular pressure and is a clear indication of their disorder. It will give you better understanding of the debilitating condition of that child.

Bonus idea ★

It's important to remember that SEMH behaviours can appear irrational and disproportionate to the external stimulation. Events such as cancelling a football match or poor test results can be disappointing to a any child but to our SEMH pupils, they can appear catastrophic.

There is hope

'Mad, sad or bad?'

Children with SEMH are neither mad, sad nor bad; they have a disability. Remaining hopeful is essential.

If you accept that SEMH pupils have a disability, then dealing with it might increase your empathy and improve your understanding of some of the dreadful behaviours they display. It's that persistence of the unwanted behaviours that identifies them as SEMH.

But there is hope, if you take a holistic approach to your classroom and child management. By creating a good environment, you can change the behaviour.

Over the course of my teaching career, I have shadowed classes for a whole day. Each new teacher presents a new environment with varied expectations and demands. What shocked me was how the class and the child with SEMH changed their behaviour for different teachers – from almost rioting in one classroom to calm and attentive in another. When the class went from disorder to order, or vice versa, the change occurred immediately when the new teacher took over. Better management did not cure the child's problems but they were manageable and teaching took place. The more the SEMH child experiences an appropriate environment, the more the disability is reduced. Good management in school with increased positive rewarding can also have a positive effect on home behaviour.

You will still not be able to turn SEMH pupils into model pupils by managing all aspects of the environment. However, you can give them hope by creating aspects of their school experience that are rewarding.

Coping with escalation

Part 10

Escalation

'If a crisis is managed adequately, it has a very positive effect on teacher, class and child.'

Kaplan and Wheeler's cycle of assault suggests the following pattern: trigger followed by escalation to crisis phase, then (if resolved) on to recovery phase and finally post-crisis depression phase. If you keep that sequence in mind, you will be more capable of managing the crisis phase, which may contain a physical threat.

Let's look at the cycle of assault in detail:

- The **trigger** phase involves you in observation, negotiation and interventions.
- The **escalation** phase requires de-escalation techniques which means careful observation and measuring of the pupil's level of instability.
- The **crisis** phase may require physical management or physical prompting to remove the child from the classroom.
- The **recovery** phase requires counselling and settling the pupil. Be careful here: it is not the end of the incident.
- The **post-crisis** phase requires a safe place to calm down. It should not be a time for punishment or harsh words.

This clear model of what you may face is a predictable pattern. However, like all aspects of working with SEMH pupils, it is not always possible to predict their behaviour. For example, a child may move directly from trigger to crisis, so be prepared.

Kaplan, S.G. and Wheeler, E.G. (1983), 'Survival skills for working with potentially violent clients'. *Social Casework*, 64, 6, 339–346.

Clear warnings of trouble

'Always keep an eye on small difficult behaviours.'

Spotting early signals of distress can help you avoid a crisis.

When the pupil makes life unmanageable for you and the class, they reach a state of such anxiety and stress that the only possible outlet for their feelings is rapid escalation. Most escalations start with initial warnings of intent. These can include: silence and withdrawal; refusing a simple request; refusing eye contact; ignoring a demand; and erratic, repetitive noise-making. Beware: these behaviours can be clear warnings of the child's mental state.

With these pre-escalation behaviours, the child is displaying to you their inability to manage the immediate environment. Other marginal pupils may encourage the disturbed behaviour, increasing the chances of a rapid escalation.

When you spot these signals, try to get the challenging child either into a safe place or out of the room altogether. Don't refer to their behaviour; the pupil is already aware of what is happening. Find an excuse for the distressed child to leave the classroom with a TA, e.g. a visit to the library or collecting something from the head's office. Getting out of the situation can help slow life down for a bit. Once the child is calm, they can come back into the classroom. It might appear a bit drastic to send the child out of the classroom (well, it is), but if you allow the distress to flower then it becomes more difficult for you to manage the behaviour on your own and you may need the senior management team to resolve not only the immediate problem but the consequential damage incurred.

Teaching tip

This idea assumes you have managed this pupil before, and will be aware of the extremes of behaviour the child can exhibit. The quicker you can intervene, the better the prognosis. However, you need to be careful: be quiet, not loud; move slowly, not quickly; no fast talking; and use clear uncluttered instruction.

Raised voice vs shouting

'Don't shout, but raise your voice when required.'

Losing your temper and shouting will never help a difficult situation, but the careful use of a raised voice can have a positive effect.

What is the difference between a teacher raising their voice and shouting? Just pause and think about this question for a minute before you read on.

Raising your voice

My view is that raising your voice is a tactic you keep at the bottom of your teacher's bag for the rare occasions you need to get it out. It's simply lifting your voice above your usual calm delivery and signalling your displeasure.

It can be delivered in many ways: close to, but not in the child's face; a few feet away; or from across the room. You might even fold your arms and look quite stern (but not angry – there is a difference). A raised voice can also be used to halt a behaviour that may have health and safety issues.

Raising your voice can be used alongside some of the tactics already suggested in this book. You have to make a judgment about the appropriateness of raising your voice, as sometimes it can light the touch paper and cause further issues.

Shouting

Shouting is a full-blown burst of verbiage at a high decibel level. It can range over more than one sentence and be used to bully or intimidate a child. It is rarely effective and can be frightening, not just for the child with SEMH but also for other children in the class. In terms of the cycle of assault (Idea 67), it can drive a child from trigger to crisis without passing go!

How hard do you push?

'Assess the situation, calculate your ability to manage it, and act.'

When a behaviour is not responding to your interventions and is either defiantly persisting or beginning to heat up, you have to decide what course of action you might take.

If it's not possible to remove the child from the classroom (Idea 74), there are several ways the situation might develop:

1 The child agrees to your demands and settles down.
2 The child thinks, 'I'm not going to go over the top here but will continue to be a big pain in the classroom.'
3 Everything blows and the child starts threatening you or another child. Behaviour can include damaging school equipment or throwing objects likely to cause harm.

Now let's think about what you can do in these situations.

Behaviour 1: This *can* happen but be watchful after the child appears to settle down – just a spark can rekindle the fire.

Behaviour 2: This is a complicated one to manage because the child is waiting for you to act. 'Come on,' they are saying to you. 'What are you going to do about ME?' It's almost like a game. The child is wound up and doesn't want to calm down but is not that keen on taking it all the way.

Behaviour 3: The child has lost control of themselves and just wants to harm people or damage objects.

Well, there's a conundrum! What are you going to do? You have to do something to de-escalate the situation but do you:

> **Teaching tip**
>
> You have watched the situation develop, you know how far the child might push you and you should know how capable you are of managing the child's distress. Think, calculate and act according to those two assessments. Impulsivity on your part will only turn up the heat.

- Go in hard, demanding obedience?
- Get close, and request that the behaviour stops?
- Risk physically prompting the child out of the room?
- Clear the classroom, leaving just you and the child?

The choice you make is more about you than the child. You have to know your limits and capabilities. You should also be aware of how far this individual is likely to take it. The next few ideas will guide you.

Demand obedience

'This is where you need to be skilful, clever and crafty.'

Going in hard and demanding obedience is a high-level skill. It requires good timing, authority, persistence, an awareness of your capabilities and sure-footedness. Once your words or actions start, you can't take them back.

If the child has now reached a level of anxiety that is difficult to step back from, you have to deal with it, because teaching has become impossible. So, what might happen? Well, so much depends on you.

Going in hard *could* cool the situation but could create a much bigger problem. The SEMH pupil has set up the stage for you to join the play but hasn't yet written your script. Going in hard might not be what the child expects and they may be surprised by your abruptness and consequently could calm down. If this happens, it would be a good idea to send them out for a cooling-down walk with a TA.

However, your unexpected, demanding response could feel almost like an assault and the pupil may defend themselves by raising the stakes. You didn't blow out the match and you lit the blue touch paper. The behaviour could now move straight to the next stage – crisis.

Teaching tip

The response you make is down to intuition, experience and confidence. There's more about the mechanics of confrontation later on in the book (Part 11).

Get close

'Decide where you are going to stand, and quietly go there.'

Getting close and requesting that the unwanted behaviour stops is like dancing with the SEMH child while the whole class is watching. Your skills are crucial and you need to identify where to stand.

Teaching tip

The space between you and the child is crucial because it signals your intent. The closer you are, the more demanding you can be. Stepping back when things go well signals the demand has been satisfied.

The unwanted behaviour has to stop, so let's look at a less confrontational response than the one in Idea 71.

Judging proximity

The class is watching how you are going to achieve a return to a calm teaching environment. You have to be close to the disruptive child, but how close? *You* have to make the judgment regarding proximity to the child. If you are too far away, it's difficult to have significant impact. If you are too close, it might be threatening. You also have to be aware of other children in the vicinity.

Speaking to the child

Your words have to be carefully chosen and the tone of your voice should be clear and low key. The child will listen very carefully to what you say. They will look for any word or phrase that can be used to maintain the belligerent behaviour. The child wants to continue the interaction but you, with carefully chosen words and phrases, can manage the child's anxiety. Change your behaviour: either keep still, move closer or perhaps step back, and see what effect that has. If a particular word or a phrase reduces the child's behaviour, use it again. Don't threaten but be very clear about what you want. A short period of silence can be a sign that things might be just cooling off. If so, gradually move away.

Physically prompt the child

'This is a high-risk strategy: think before you act, or don't act.'

Be confident about your ability to physically prompt a child out of the classroom. You must be trained and physically capable of dealing with the child you are managing – no risk-taking.

When the child is persisting in disturbing your teaching despite your interventions, you could go straight into the option of physical prompting if you have been trained.

Part of your training should include the assessment of when to act and the safe management of such an intervention. It should not be a big, powerful statement, e.g. 'I am removing you [the child]'. Instead, you should aim to keep your tone and language low key, e.g. 'This can't go on. Let's talk about it outside the classroom.' This now presents the child with a dilemma. Should they just blow the whole thing, refuse to move and see what happens or do as they are asked?

The most difficult outcome in this scenario is if the child refuses to move. If you have asked the child to talk about the problem outside the classroom, then the child *has* to leave the classroom. It would be easy to forget that you asked them to leave, but it's important that you don't back off. Instead, get yourself ready for the next stage. Say something like, 'I have asked you to leave the classroom. If you don't do as I ask, I will have to help you leave the classroom.' Note the use of the word *help* – it suggests negotiation, not force. Now is the time to stay still – no words, just wait. The child is calculating; you should appear calm. They have to decide to go down a notch and leave the room or escalate to a conflict. Whatever the child decides – to blow or to comply – they *must* leave the classroom.

Teaching tip

Only start on the road to physical management if you can be assured of the safety of all concerned and there is back-up support immediately available. Remember: unless you have been trained and are confident with physical management, you should not attempt this strategy.

Taking it further

You should be prepared in case the child chooses to blow and the situation in the classroom escalates further. This may be a time to request help from senior management.

Clear the classroom

'Clearing the class has pros and cons.'

Moving a whole class out of a room should only be used when damage to pupils, staff or property is likely.

This strategy can help you manage the situation during those times when a child has lost control of themselves and just wants to harm people or objects. I have seen this tactic used before but I am not really sure about it. There are some perspectives for you to consider in the table below.

If you have used this tactic and found it successful, I would ask at what cost? Is it a final straw? What image does the rest of the class have of the SEMH child during these times? What message do the class take home to their parents? Is it a tactic you could repeat often? What would you learn from it?

Pros	Cons
<ul><li>It takes away the audience.</li><li>It is a good safety measure for the rest of the class.</li><li>It takes away the marginal children who can be difficult at these times.</li></ul>	<ul><li>It gives the pupil with SEMH a sense of power: 'All the class are having to leave, because of ME!'</li><li>They might take advantage when the whole class is mobile.</li><li>The empty stage might be more difficult to manage.</li><li>You are not a teacher anymore. You now have a one-to-one – is that what you want?</li><li>The class is not being taught at all.</li></ul>

No hesitation, no deviation

'Don't change your demands. Stay firm.'

When a distressed pupil reaches the crisis stage, you must be clear about what is required. Start with a small request — don't go for the big change of behaviour first. Don't compromise on the initial demand.

If the child is escalating or is in crisis, you have to be rock solid and not waver or deviate from the task of resolving the problem. Once you embark on managing crisis behaviour, your expectations regarding the outcome must remain consistent.

From the beginning of the escalation, gather information from the words the child is using. Think about their manner of speech. Are they swearing? Are they using sexualised language or shouting about injustice? Check out the child's body posture too. Do they have tight fists, high shoulders or big eyes? Is their face reddening? Use that information to decide upon the tactic you are going to use.

There must be no great deviation or massive changes of expectation; you must not say 'no' to behaviour and then allow it. If you want a pupil to sit down, then eventually that must be achieved. You should not lower your expectations because that shows a crack, a weakness that will be played upon. Stand tall and be quietly confident in your attitude but keep your expectations consistent and predictable.

Think carefully about the targets you set during an escalation or crisis. If you set a behaviour target, e.g. 'no swearing', then, for the behaviour to be resolved, you must achieve clean speech. A more achievable target might be 'less swearing'.

Teaching tip

Don't start by demanding something that might be too difficult for the child to accede to. Request a small, manageable adjustment. Keep calm and wait for the next opportunity to ask for another small adjustment. If the distressed child does not respond favourably to even the slightest request for change, then they are beyond negotiation. See Part 11 for more help.

You are in a crisis

'Stay calm, be clear and resolute.'

Maintain good body posture, appear calm, speak clearly and don't muddle your words. You are in a crisis situation and the child is watching and listening to everything.

When SEMH pupils are escalating towards crisis, it is important that you get the style and tone of your speech correct. Any inappropriate remark or too heavy an emphasis on obedience can cause a major disruption. See Idea 61 for more advice.

You may have mannerisms that suggest you are anxious, such as playing with your watch or rolling up your sleeves. Keep such mannerisms in check and avoid repetitive movements. A child in crisis will be watching you for any sign that suggests that they have the upper hand.

- Keep as relaxed as possible.
- Check your shoulders and keep them dropped and loose.
- Keep your arms loose and by your side.
- Try not to flap your hands about.
- Keep your back straight.
- Don't bend down to talk to the child.

Back up

'If you think you can't manage the behaviour, get help.'

The moment you feel a situation is slipping away from you, get help. No bravery, no heroics — timing is of the essence, so don't delay.

If behaviour becomes physically dangerous during the escalation phase then follow only agreed procedures. There should be a protocol in the school that gives an immediate response to physical danger. If you don't know the protocol in your school, find out as soon as you can.

The most crucial point of any call-out procedure is 'when?'. You must anticipate when behaviour is beginning to slip away from your control. That's the time to bring in support. Too early might exacerbate the problem; too late and the force required is that much greater and the destruction more significant.

Remember: the decision to call out support is not a sign of your incompetence but is more about the level of turbulence inside the child with SEMH.

Taking it further

Here are some questions to ask at the end of the day when everything has calmed down: Could I have intervened earlier? Did I do something to make the situation worse? Did the violence excite other pupils in the class? Did I do things to the best of my ability and did the situation still become dangerous?

Mightier than the sword

'You can sometimes halt a behaviour by just writing down what is happening.'

This idea can stop a situation getting out of hand and give you time to think. Try it; you might be surprised.

When a pupil reaches crisis stage, their behaviour can, at times, be strange and bizarre. They often say and do things that are unusual – almost surreal. For example, they might make sexualised remarks about you, your mother, your father or the headteacher. They seem to be completely oblivious to the consequences of what they say or do.

Move quietly towards the troubled child with paper and pen or a tablet and start to write down what is being said. Also describe the behaviour out loud and write it down. The child will often react by asking you what you are doing. Now you have an excellent opportunity to start a conversation about what is being said and what is being acted out. Most importantly, the child will be concerned about the consequence of you writing it all down.

By writing down what is said, you are creating a record of what is happening, and that in itself is a consequence. This can often have a significant effect on the child's behaviour; they now know there will be a record for all to see and that might prove difficult when all is quiet again.

Big time trouble – crisis

Part 11

Resist shouting

'Get closer slowly – no rushing. Don't bump into furniture; plot your pathway towards the distressed child. Be aware of the risks to other pupils and adults.'

Remain conscious of the messages your posture and language send to the child as they enter crisis.

At crisis times, a level of frustration can set in that the child cannot resolve. The triggers that have contributed to the crisis now become more invasive and potentially more dangerous. Without shouting but with a strong voice and a good body posture, you must convey calmness and control.

Speech
- Be conscious of your breathing; take slow, deep breaths, which allow longer periods of speaking.
- Avoid running out of breath mid-sentence. The distressed child will pick that up and read it as stress.
- Talk slowly and calmly about the situation the child has placed themselves in. Be direct but not aggressive.

Posture
- Keep your body tall and check that your shoulders are relaxed; people have a tendency to lift their shoulders when threatened and this can be negatively rewarding for the distressed pupil.
- Don't clench your fists but keep your hands loose and calm by your side.
- Avoid stumbles or trips and be aware of any hazards to movement.

If you get these behaviours right, it makes you feel more confident about your ability to deal with serious incidents and improves your performance.

No threats, no ultimatums

'When a crisis occurs, you must maintain objectivity.'

When pupils with SEMH push you hard, you can be forced into corners and some responses can be close to ultimatums or threats. These ultimatums can be said in the heat of the moment and regretted for the rest of your teaching career.

The phrases to avoid include:

- If you do that I will...
- Do that again and I will...
- Stop that or I will...
- Now you have done that, I will have to...

These phrases can be changed into:

- It might be better not to do that because...
- It would be silly to do that again because it would make things worse...
- If you could stop doing that then perhaps we could...
- You know what happens when you do that. Would it not be better to perhaps...?

Taking away the threat or ultimatum leaves room for negotiation and prevents the pupil from feeling trapped. You are seen in a good light by the rest of the class and, as a consequence, they are far more likely to support you. Getting them on your side weighs heavily with children in distress – they may sense that things are going against them and may retreat.

Teaching tip

When a distressed child starts to shout, you can feel pressured. They can shout and demand, and you might feel that you need to shout and demand too. In most cases, it just sends the child over the top and creates a bigger problem.

Eyeball to eyeball!

'No wavering; eyeball to eyeball, no blinking.'

Eye contact can be crucial during crisis time; if you can maintain eye contact, you can project a sense of control and confidence.

When more profound behaviour erupts, it is essential that you appear calm and composed. This is a skill you must try to master. Although the behaviour may not be directed at you, it is your authority that is being flouted.

When communicating in any way with a distressed pupil, it is important to maintain full, uninterrupted eye contact. You must maintain a strong, unblinking, calm gaze – no narrowing, tightening and no expression, just clear and steady.

By using strong eye contact at these crucial times, you are showing your lack of fear and expressing your position as the authority in the room – you are confronting the child's wish to take control.

Maintaining constant, unshakable eye contact is difficult. Try this powerful tactic on less difficult pupils and see how they respond.

Teaching tip

Don't look directly into their eyes, but look instead at the bridge of their nose. That's easier for you, as you're not challenged by their eye contact, but they think you're looking directly into their eyes. Try it out with a friend.

Bonus idea ★

Without warning, try unblinking eye-to-eye contact on a partner, relative or close friend. Ask them how it felt and work on the tactic with them. Check out your eyes in a mirror and see how long you can stare without blinking. Make sure you don't open your mouth or lower or raise your eyebrows. Keep a steady face and remember: NO blinking.

Maybe a touch can quell the fire?

'Just a gentle touch can have a positive effect on the child's state of mind.'

Light physical contact such as touching the back of the hand can reduce some children's anxiety.

When a pupil reaches a heightened anxiety state, they feel isolated and peripheral to the class and this can lead them to feel a sense of rejection. This is not surprising as it is mostly true. All these feelings are adding to the child's arousal and need to be taken into account.

If you can get close to the distressed pupil, it might be advisable to attempt light physical contact. This *has* to be done with caution and should, in most cases, be looked upon as a thermometer to test the child's anxiety levels. The only safe areas at this stage are the upper and lower arm and the back of the hand – touching any other area could be misunderstood. **If the reaction to any kind of touch is quite violent or rejecting, do not try it again.**

However, if the child doesn't react negatively to light physical contact or perhaps accepts it, then you have made considerable progress. Wait briefly for confirmation of acceptance – which may come in the form of a less aggressive tone or a less aggressive statement of the perceived problem – then remove your hand. Repeat the physical contact if reconciliation appears to be starting. Don't proceed to more invasive physical contact as this could be perceived as something other than comfort, i.e. threat.

Teaching tip

At no time in this process should any hold or grip be placed on the pupil unless you have been trained in restraint and are confident about the methods you use.

Distraction techniques

'Give distraction a chance; it can work, I assure you.'

This intervention isn't a magic cure, but can bring the temperature down a bit without a cross word. It doesn't resolve the crisis but it is an opportunity to communicate at a lower level. If it decreases the temperature, you could be on the way to a quieter time.

If a child is angry, silent and ready to explode, try taking your intervention away from the immediate and mention something that might appear irrelevant to the situation you are facing. Here are some example phrases you could use:

- I haven't seen you wear those shoes before.
- Like your new pen.
- Your voice sounds a bit rough, have you got a cold?
- Liverpool did well last night.
- Did you see (whatever) on telly last night? I know you like that programme.
- Mr Johnson said you played well in the practice match.
- Are you feeling cold? Shall we get your coat?

Sometimes this distracts from the crisis and gives the child a chance to step back from the edge. It doesn't end there, but can slow down the escalation and lead on to a conversation about the real issue with slightly less heat.

Calm insistence on just one behaviour

'Pick a request and stick to it.'

During a crisis, be a broken record about just *one* behaviour.

If you get this tactic right at times of crisis, it works really well, but you have to use it carefully and sparingly.

There can be challenging times in a crisis when things narrow down to two or three quite distinct difficulties. These can include shouting, abuse, swearing, shoving furniture, threatening, moving around the room or making loud noises. Select one challenge to resolve and just acknowledge the others. Quietly and repeatedly confront just your chosen behaviour. Keep referring to it often, using the same words over and over again. For example, in a situation where the child is swearing, shouting demands and moving around the room, you might like to focus on the movement: 'Okay, I understand that but please just sit. (Pause.) Yes, I will deal with that as well but please just sit down. (Pause.) That's fine but just sit down please.' Remain insistent but don't get angry. You should give credit to other problems, but keep to the task. Keep calm, be clear and stick to your guns because if you choose the right behaviour at the right time, it does work.

This tactic will help you gain some control over a small part of a much larger problem. By acknowledging all the other outrages, demands and threats but selecting one single behaviour to work on, you are giving to the child an opportunity to comply. The pupil is internally bubbling away and out of control, but a request to comply on a single issue may feel like a way out of the fury.

Safety first

'Make sure you know what you can and can't do.'

When some SEMH pupils reach a crisis that has not been resolved in the escalation phase, your first consideration should be the safety of the child, other pupils and adults in the class.

See below the Department for Education's statement (2013) on the use of reasonable force.

'Schools can use reasonable force to:

- remove disruptive children from the classroom where they have refused to follow an instruction to do so;
- prevent a pupil behaving in a way that disrupts a school event or a school trip or visit;
- prevent a pupil leaving the classroom where allowing the pupil to leave would risk their safety or lead to behaviour that disrupts the behaviour of others;
- prevent a pupil from attacking a member of staff or another pupil, or to stop a fight in the playground; and
- restrain a pupil at risk of harming themselves through physical outbursts.'

If a child requires the use of reasonable force on a regular basis, it is advisable to undertake a certificated course on the use of reasonable force with an accredited organisation. This can help you by reducing the risk of the child or other children in the vicinity being harmed.

When having to restrain a child, it is important for teachers to have a protocol to follow. If the child requires physical prompting out of the room, it is necessary for the teacher to be confident that the hold used is safe for the child. If other children are close, they should also be safe from damage or injury.

Physically dangerous behaviour

'Think quickly and act according to previous experiences.'

If the child's behaviour becomes physically dangerous then follow only agreed procedures. There should be a protocol in the school that gives an immediate response to physical danger.

The most crucial point of the call-out procedure is the point at which you must decide that the child's behaviour is slipping away from your control. If you are no longer in control, then it's time to bring in support. Too early might exacerbate the problem; too late and the force required is that much greater and the destruction more significant.

It is important to consider the history of the child and your relationship with them when behaviour becomes physically dangerous. When dealing with a child at this extreme level of anxiety, ask yourself:

- Does the pupil have a history of violence?
- Have I felt anxious for my safety with this pupil before?
- Has their behaviour followed similar patterns before and what was the outcome?
- Could I have intervened earlier?
- Did I do something to make the situation worse?
- Are other pupils in the class getting excited by the violence?
- Did I do things to the best of my ability and did it still become dangerous?

There are obviously many more questions you could ask; add them to the list and keep the prompt available to scan if things get very difficult.

Teaching tip

When behaviour has become physically dangerous, you should call for back up. See Idea 77 for more information.

Calming right down

Part 12

De-escalating

'How you handle de-escalation is crucial. Don't rush it, and take notes.'

When a child has been removed from the classroom, the school should make arrangements for the teacher to manage the de-escalation. Ideally, it should take place in appropriate and quiet surroundings.

Consider health and safety. Make sure there are no objects around that the child might use as a weapon and no irritating distractions that might cause the child to react negatively. If you give the child a cup of tea, make sure the tea is cool enough to handle or put it in a special container that won't spill.

If you work carefully through the de-escalation phase successfully, the benefits can be significant. Successful de-escalation can reduce the chances of the crisis occurring again. The troubled pupil may talk about what *really* caused the crisis. In some cases, the child may make disclosures of abuse. There can be guilt (we all know how corrosive that can be, so better out than in). There can also be reconciliation.

When moving a distressed pupil, always keep to the procedures laid down by the school. Moving them out of the classroom will disturb the child, but this next phase of calming down is crucial. The child should be moved to a quiet place, with no aggravating elements that might hinder calming. The child might still be distressed and some form of physical management might be required.

Speak quietly, listen carefully and don't rush into conversation until the child stops some of the aggressive behaviour. They might take a while to acclimatise to the new environment – give them time.

As tempers reduce, begin to talk through the event. You could take a few notes, especially if the child is able to talk through the incident. Just wait, make no judgment and certainly do not talk of punishment.

If possible, sit close to the child and carefully release any restraint that may have been required. Offer a drink if the child calms down sufficiently – even a cup of tea with a bit of sugar in it. Some might think that this is 'rewarding bad behaviour' but, in fact, it's rewarding good behaviour – the child is quiet.

Peace time

'Make sure the child really is calm and quiet.'

Once the child has settled down after an incident, allow some time for a period of quiet. The best place for this is a room with few people.

A corner of the headteacher's office or the SENCO's room, or perhaps even the staffroom when everybody is teaching, can all be used as spaces to let the child calm down – it all depends on availability.

During the peace time, no words have to be spoken (especially about the crisis phase) – just let the child's mind clear the anger, and get back a normal speaking voice and a less tense body. A normal conversation may be held about, for example, the football, a TV programme, or whatever interesting object or painting there may be on the wall. Don't let these conversations go on too long; the child is not to be entertained, just quietly maintained in a safe place.

If the problems of the crisis period are mentioned by the child, just listen and, where possible, change the conversation. This quiet time is to loosen the muscles and relax the mind. If the child mentions the crisis, they are not ready to return to the class because, inside their head, something is still bubbling away. Returning to the classroom could cause the bubbles to increase.

There is nothing better than boredom to encourage the child back to class. The pupil knows what's going on elsewhere as the odd sound will filter through from classrooms or even the corridor.

Teaching tip

This engineered time of peace is an essential part of de-escalation, so don't try to cut corners here. Check the child's speech – is it back to normal? Does the child have a quiet body, no tics, no fidgeting?

Release after de-escalation

'It is essential that re-entry is safe and trouble-free.'

Once the distressed child is calm and quiet, they can be released back to the class. Be careful: this can be a risky time, even if the tea and talk have been successful and a period of peace has been experienced.

Time the re-entry to the classroom at the beginning of the next phase of teaching. Make sure the work given matches the child's capabilities. If there is work to finish from the crisis period, you could give the child time to complete it. You have to be careful regarding the request to complete work missed due to a crisis – only do so if the work is not too difficult and was not the cause of the escalation.

If the pupil has calmed down, towards the end of the day, go through what occurred earlier and discuss it. Remember that the pupil has experienced a traumatic time and needs to feel that they have made reparation in some way for earlier behaviour.

End the session on a positive note. A calmer interchange between you and the pupil will make a recurrence of the crisis the following day less likely. These tiny positive times can also establish a warmer relationship between you and the child.

Remember: it's all about rebalancing your relationship with the child.

Reparation

'Reparation is far more powerful than punishment.'

When you are confident that the anger and stress have reduced sufficiently for discussions to take place regarding damage, then you could start talking about repair and reparation.

It must depend on the severity of the damage and abuse, but (if carefully managed) reparation can often be a turning point with more sensitive pupils. Although they may not appear sensitive, SEMH children can be affected quite significantly by damage they might have caused.

There are several ways you can manage this by suggesting, for example, that they:

- help put the classroom back together
- repair, with your help, any furniture that may have been damaged
- glue back together any damaged books or displays
- help a fellow pupil who might have been hurt or frightened by the incident
- make apologies to any other adult or pupil who might have found the incident distressing.

Most of this reparation should be done in private, away from the gaze of other children who might find the repair or apology amusing.

If there is any significant damage to the classroom or school equipment, involve the child in the repair. If the damage requires the purchase of a replacement, go through the reordering process with the child.

Taking it further

If the crisis caused another child to be frightened or hurt in the incident, at an appropriate time, arrange a chat between the SEMH pupil and those others who were affected.

IDEA 91

Safeguarding

'Too many serious incidents means something is badly wrong.'

If a particular child causes more than one serious incident over a short period of time, e.g. two in a week, then questions should be asked about WHY this behaviour is repeating.

A discussion with a member of the SLT or SENCO might be helpful. To gain insight into the child's frame of mind, questions should be asked about what *caused* the incidents.

Firstly, look at the dynamics in the classroom that might cause such significant behaviours:

- Is the teacher stressed by the behaviour and consequently reacting inappropriately to the child?
- Are the dynamics of the class unbalanced?
- Is there any significant bullying of the child occurring in the class or elsewhere in the school?

Secondly, ask yourself whether there is any evidence of significant stress at home:

- Have any new adults been introduced to the household?
- Is the child marked in any way?
- Is the child using more sexualised language?

A simple rule is that if a child needs to be restrained or causes significant damage to school property twice in a five-day cycle, the parent should be asked to come into the school to discuss the matter. Significant behaviours not only take up a great deal of resources but also prevent access to the curriculum for the rest of the class.

If it's not
working, analyse

Part 13

Recording individual behaviours

'Clear, objective data can give insight into what might be seen as chaos.'

When, what, where, at what time and with whom? All these are important factors when describing a behaviour.

Design a shorthand for the difficult behaviours a child presents to you as a class manager. Here's an example from my own practice:

Behaviour description	Code
Not on task	not
Annoying another pupil	aap
Shouting at teacher or TA	sat
Out of seat	oos
Running out of room	room
Shouting at another pupil	sap
Pushing a teacher or TA	ptt
Pushing another pupil	pap

In a table or record sheet, record the time of the incident, in which subject it occurred and who else was involved. Deal with the problem, make a brief note and move on. At the end of the day, add some brief notes about your observation. Here is an example of pupil RR's behaviour:

Time	Behaviour	Subject	Other people involved
9.00	not	Quiet reading	Trying to attract JS's attention.
10.00	oos	English	Asked to sit down: went back past JS.
11.00	sap	After break	RR and JS had a fight; started with name calling.
12.30	pap	Lunch	Pushing and name calling JS on the playground.
1.00	oos	Quiet reading	Wandering near JS, TA puts RR back in seat.
2.00	pap	Topic	Talked with RR and JS outside classroom.
3.00	sat	Free choice	Shouting 'You never do anything about JS'; RR ran out.
4.00	sat	Home time	A chat with RR and suggested we talk to mum.

Using your data

'I try to capture everything, but the most important thing is using the information to my advantage.'

Once you've got an overview of what's happening, what can you do with the data you've collected?

Once you start recording incidents – major and minor – you will begin to see what the triggers are and can start to build a managing strategy to improve the child's behaviour.

Look back at the behaviour record in Idea 92. If you were faced with this situation, you could use your data to determine how to act. Here are some suggestions to consider:

- You could change when the pupils go out to break.
- You could make sure JS sits away from RR.
- You might meet RR and JS at breaktimes for a chat.
- You could get them to play a supervised board game to improve their relationship.
- Write a simple reward scheme, which both children have to sign up to, and send it home to both sets of parents.

Teaching tip

Keeping an individual record of a child's behaviour gives a clear, timed record of what *actually* happened. You have a database that you can refer to. You might discover that original behaviours have reduced considerably.

IDEA 94

Is a particular child THAT difficult?

'Make a comparison between *your* perception of a child and the perceptions of other staff who have contact.'

The severity of the behaviour a particular child with SEMH displays is not that easy to define. Different managing adults can see the same pupil in entirely different ways. Use this idea to find out which adults are having the most positive impact.

One teacher may find pupil A easy to teach while another may find the same child difficult. This suggests that an adult handling pupil A in a different way reduces disruption.

The difference in perception of pupil A can be problematic. How can the school identify the level of dysfunction of an individual pupil who is 'good' with one adult and 'difficult' with another? One question to ask is, 'Is a pupil's level of dysfunction related to the individual adult's skills?' Contrasting management skills are not uncommon in schools and it can be very uncomfortable for adults who are finding life difficult to realise that others do not share their experiences with a particular child.

One objective way of looking at this common problem might be to ask the adults working with pupil A to complete a behaviour assessment form. Ask at least five adults to complete the form. **Strictly no conferring between adults.** Once all the assessments have been completed, compare the results.

This simple behaviour assessment is not a weighty document but could be a guide to pupil A's response to certain adults. The results can be used to share adult perception of specific pupils and the way they are managed. The outcomes can be used as a guide to what works and what doesn't.

Teaching tip

The behaviour assessment form is a critique of the adult's management skills with a disruptive pupil. Objectively comparing the skills of all adults and identifying what works and what doesn't can reduce disruption in the classroom.

Bonus idea ★

Take the behaviour assessment at set intervals to see whether changes in management are successful. A SENCO working with this group of adults can coach responses that are more appropriate and eradicate others that simply make the behaviour worse!

128

Behaviour assessment form								
Name _____**Class** _____ **Date** ___/ ___/ ___								
EMOTIONS	**1**	**2**	**3**	**4**	**5**			**Score**
Happy, contented						Unhappy, anxious		
Copes easily with new situations/people						Difficult with new situations/people		
Even-tempered, easy-going						Irritable, quarrelsome		
Positive self-image						Negative self-image		
Total								
LEARNING	**1**	**2**	**3**	**4**	**5**			**Score**
Concentrates well, not easily distracted						Cannot concentrate on task, distractible		
Eager to learn, curious, contented						Shows little curiosity, no work motivation		
Perseveres if work is difficult/challenging						Lacks perseverance with work		
Can work independently						Needs constant help and encouragement		
Total								
CONDUCT	**1**	**2**	**3**	**4**	**5**			**Score**
Helpful, considerate towards others						Bullies or is spiteful towards others		
Sociable, friendly						Solitary, withdrawn		
Readily accepts discipline and control						Generally disruptive or disobedient		
Can ignore difficult behaviour						Joins in disruption		
Total								
COMMENTS							**Total score**	

Sharing skills

'Talk openly about your management of a pupil to other members of staff.'

If a teacher is really struggling with a class or a particular pupil, what can you or the school do about it? This is an essential question to ask, but not an easy one to answer.

As seen in Idea 94, measuring a pupil's behaviour is not straightforward because children's behaviour may change in relation to the adult's skills. This suggests that some teachers are better than others with SEMH pupils (I think most teachers would agree with that). Teachers do not all have the same skill levels or experience, nor do they have the same ability to manage stress and conflict.

Peer observation can help all parties. No big chunks of time are required – perhaps 15–30 minutes. You could use a structured observation sheet like the one on the next page.

Make the observations once per minute. Start by observing and noting the behaviour of the child with SEMH, then the whole class and finally the teacher. Give some time at the beginning of the lesson to allow the class to settle and a bit of time at the end to just scan the class.

Structured observation sheets are more objective and give a sound basis on which to talk later. You could start by getting a group of three or four teachers to observe each other. Meet together at the end of the week to compare notes and identify what different approaches were observed. Each teacher can compare how colleagues manage whole classes and use interventions. A SENCO could be involved or even a member of the SLT.

Timed observation sheet (15 minutes)

Period	SEMH pupil	Whole class	Teacher	Teacher positive? (Tick)	Teacher negative? (Tick)
1	OOS	LTT	TWC	✓	
2					
3					
...					

Here are some common codes that cover a range of different behaviours.

SEMH behaviour codes

TOT   talking out of turn
NOT   not on task
ON   on task
OOS   out of seat
BD   being disruptive
MN   making noises

Class behaviour codes

LTT   listening to teacher
AOT   all on task
NOT   more than 50% not on task
LOM   lots of movement
MN   making noises

Teacher behaviour codes

TWC   talking to whole class
WA   walking around
WIP   working with individual pupil
WSG   working with small group
TOR   teacher out of room
WDC   working with SEMH child

Don't panic, learn

'We learn more from our mistakes than our successes.'

Losing control of a difficult child happens to all of us. The trick is to learn from the mistakes you make. Experiment, expand your repertoire and don't panic.

Get a trusted colleague to sit in your class and watch you teach. Listen carefully to their comments and take them on board. Later, ask them to sit with you again and listen to the new observations they make. Here's an analogy: say someone finds driving in London traffic stressful. Sit beside them and see how they drive. Then, after a discussion drive with them again and see how it goes. As their skills improve, their stress levels should reduce and their driving should improve. Perhaps the most significant change might be to avoid panicking when things get difficult.

Managing children with SEMH is a bit like driving. Here are some tips for you to reflect on:

- You have to set up the classroom carefully.
- Don't rush; teach at the right speed.
- Keep scanning, noting what all the children are doing.
- Know where you are going and what your targets are.
- If things get difficult, brake and review.
- Know when to change direction.
- If a child starts to push, think carefully about your responses.
- Most of all, you have to **stay calm**.

Be objective

'Subjectivity is overrated; objectivity is edifying.'

It's difficult to be objective about problematic behaviour because that behaviour can be exhausting, but you have a duty to remain objective.

Your records will map the behaviour patterns in your classroom by showing:

- an objective view of what the problems in your classroom are
- how difficult the behaviours are
- how frequently they occur
- at what time of day they happen
- during which lessons they occur.

Your records will also provide a number of direct benefits:

- You can measure the SEMH children's behaviour against the rest of the class.
- You will know when their behaviours occur and how often.
- You will have a record of the class's response to the SEMH pupils' behaviour.

If you collect this information regularly, you will have real data – not tired recollections or subjective memories. As a result, you can improve your teaching programmes, sharpen your management skills, and, above all, be more objective and fairer about your SEMH pupils' problems.

While not the primary focus of the data-collection exercise, this data can be invaluable in providing evidence of the need for additional SEND support resources.

Creative ideas

'Consolidate what works and modify what doesn't. Don't blame yourself or the child. Think and analyse.'

Education is a breeding ground for ideas and that is not a bad thing. However, it's not ideas that change what we do in the classroom; it's being objective about their implementation.

I have tried in this book to write about the working practices with SEMH pupils that colleagues and I have found successful. Yes, they did start as just ideas relating to working with these children. Some did work, and worked even better when modified. Some ideas didn't work and we probably learnt more from our mistakes than the successes.

It's having the ability to learn from mistakes that I have found to be the key to developing my management of these children. To do that, I would strongly recommend a more analytical approach. You are working with chaotic children and the understanding of their chaos is the key to a happier child and a workable classroom.

This doesn't mean that you should be afraid to experiment, but don't become too dogmatic about an idea. Observing, analysing and modifying is a healthy way to raise your skill level.

Clearing your head

'Make time for yourself and your interests outside school.'

Take time to switch off after work – it's essential to look after your own mental health as well as the children's.

The vast majority of teachers are hard-working, dedicated professionals. Teachers work from the beginning to the end of the working day in an atmosphere that is rarely less than challenging; the demands of the job are clear and can appear never-ending. Then you have the added spice of a sprinkling of SEMH pupils and the associated difficulties. Then along comes a book like this one, which tells you to appear fresh as a daisy at the start, middle and end of the day.

Having taught for many years, I do know how this sometimes feels. However, you must do something to separate work and home sufficiently to give your brain and body a chance to recover. This is not just another bit of advice; it is essential. Your brain and body need to do something for an hour or so after school – go for a jog, play squash, do some knitting, paint a picture, go for a bike ride, do some elaborate cooking, even an hour's decorating (just an hour, mind – don't go mad on that as well). Don't flop in front of the telly with a bottle of wine – at least not straight after work and not until you have eaten.

This is not a joke; it's serious stuff. For your own personal wellbeing, take a break and think about YOU. Not just one day a week but every night after work. Get into a YOU routine.

> **Teaching tip**
>
> Yes, school can be extremely hard work but don't neglect yourself and your needs. Teaching all day and thinking about it all night is not healthy.

Finding the balance

'You are going to need an open mind, a chunk of perseverance and some basic skills.'

To be effective and happy in your work with SEMH pupils, you have to look for a balance between you as a person — with all your flaws and idiosyncrasies — and the person you have to construct to get the management right.

There has to be a bit of a 'false you' that you put on when you enter school; it's a role you have to play. This is not dishonest, but about being a professional.

- You have to balance what you are happy with and what is possible within the bounds of your personality.
- You must search for a way of behaving that controls all the class and allows you to teach — because that's what you get paid for.
- If you don't think creatively, you will start to blame the children and that is the road to ruin.
- If you think creatively about the job of teaching, there is every chance that you will evolve into a confident and effective professional.